ANDREW TOOGOOD

Who do you say I am?

First edition

This book was professionally typeset on Reedsy.
Find out more at reedsy.com

To Penny, Ben, Hope & Sophie.
I love you with all my heart.

Contents

Foreword

For those who don't know me I grew up as the son of one of the greatest preachers the world has ever seen. Christianity was my whole life. I have lived in and around the church from when I was born. By the time I reached my twenties, I'd listened to a countless number of sermons from some of the very best preachers from around the world. Suffice to say there was very little that could impress me, or change my view of the Christian life. In 2007 however my life was changed forever. Through the words of Pastor Joseph Prince I heard about the love of Jesus and it revolutionised my life . I heard that I am His beloved and I have never been the same since that day.

Our words have power. More importantly the words of Jesus and what He says about you have infinite power to change your life forever.

My friend Pastor Andrew Toogood has written an absolute gem. I love this book! It is down to earth, honest, practical and easy to read. It's filled with the words of Jesus and the truth of who He is. "Who do you say I am?" offers a real and honest perspective on how you can walk successfully in this world, by meditating of the words of Jesus.

After living through the pandemic, one of the things that is true is that we cannot depend on the wisdom of this world to sustain us here on earth. These past few years have been difficult. People are tired, fearful and looking for hope. Now more than ever before people need Jesus.

God is not confused. This book is perfect for the time we are living in now. He is our only hope. C.S Lewis once said "We need to be reminded more than instructed." This is what this book has been for me. It's a reminder of who Jesus is for me. You will be reminded of His love for you and how to walk in his unmerited favour and grace for your life.

Honestly, the three chapters Satisfied, I AM and Famous Last Words should be read over and over again. These chapters are pure gold. I would encourage you to take your time and meditate on these words. Feed on these personal words from Jesus. You will discover how He loves you and offers everything you need to walk in victory in this life!

Who are you depending on, leaning on, looking to and confiding in? Pastor Andrew encourages us to build our life on the only sure foundation there is - Jesus, His finished work and what He says about you.

Be blessed and enjoy!

Pastor Joshua McCauley

Global Senior Pastor - Redemption Church

www.redemptionchurch.co.za

1

Introduction

When I first had the idea of writing a book I was tempted to take the highlights from my journey so far and put them into a greatest hits of wisdom concerning life and ministry; I estimated that it would certainly not be as impressive as other's stories but I might as well make my life seem as remarkable as possible. I mean people want that don't they? People love stories of great heroes who smash through every obstacle armed with nothing but a toothpick and a shoelace. They rise each morning with nice breath, perfect hair and achieve more before breakfast than anyone else can do in a whole day. Their gorgeous partners are perfect and their children never misbehave. These heroes start churches that grow to 10,000 people in six months and never have a disagreement with anyone on the way, they do not know what it means to struggle as that is only for the weak, or those who are not as gifted. The truth however is that all of that stuff is about as genuine as an Instagram influencer's timeline. There is real pressure to pretend that we are something that we are not; it seems easier to do that as well.

So if you were searching for a self help guide with ten steps to a better you then this would be a great time to set this book down and try something else! I I often feel like my life is a roller coaster of ups and downs. I have spent more time feeling discouraged and disappointed than I would probably like to admit - as a Christian, and especially as a pastor. I wish it was not so, but there have been significant periods of my life where I have walked through times of intense challenge and struggle. Of course that is not the full story. I have also been blessed with experiences and opportunities that many others will never have, so am I not trying to paint a picture that my life is awful as that would not be true. God has blessed me richly and I am so grateful for all He does for me; but I live with this feeling that there is more for me and my family. God has not finished with me yet: I am believing that my best days, and yours, are still to come.

For many years I lived with this sense of being stuck, a feeling of living "in the now, but the not yet." A place of tension between the desire for deeper levels of purpose and a growing confidence in God's grace in my life, versus my actual experience, which often felt limited. Somehow the stories I read of bold faith and breakthrough felt like they were for others. I feared that I would never see the same. The burden of living with a sense that I needed to try harder for God was often overwhelming.

Perhaps you know what that is like too. It can be incredibly frustrating and painful to live with a gnawing sense that we rarely make the grade. We hear that God's promises are good, but often our experience suggests those same promises are not all for me. When we are not experiencing a particular promise we often process that the problem lies with us. It feeds our fear that we are not good enough. If others saw the unvarnished version of us and not the carefully curated social media image, it would be obvious to them that we are not making the mark. We can live with a strong sense of what is called Imposter Syndrome: that is the feeling that we are going to be found out for what we truly are and it is an exhausting way to live.

There is good news for you today, there is so much more goodness, hope and favour than what you are currently experiencing. You might believe that to be true in theory but the real question is "how can we experience it more fully?" One thing I have learned about life is that my best effort is woefully lacking in creating anything of real meaning and purpose. I am not enough. Thank goodness there is a better way.

This is a book about the amazing grace of Jesus and what that means for your life. Grace is God's best for you. By 'grace' I mean the unearned, undeserved and unmerited favour of Jesus.

You were never called to live a life that is anything less than full and free. That is not a pseudo self-improvement myth, but rather a promise from God Himself. He is speaking that truth over your life right now, even as you read these words. When Jesus said that He came to give you life in all of His fullness, that is exactly what He meant. He was not overstating or exaggerating, He was not playing to the crowd or trying to win favour with men. He was expressing the deepest desire of God to see you live in the fullness of every promise that was ever given by Him. We will only ever live that way through His grace as there is no way we can 'perform our way' into His favour.

And therein lies the tension for us today: what we know God has spoken over us, against the inconsistent way our lives often play out.

What do you do when your days are falling short of what Jesus says is His heart's desire for you and for your family? Where do you look for comfort when the challenges are real and pressing? When your health fails, when paying the bills is a stretch and relationships are broken?

What do the promises of God mean to you in those moments? When we are under pressure we are prone to ask the wrong question; let me explain:

Penny and I had been married for a few years whenever we encountered our first big challenge as a couple. We married quite young and had a few fun years building our first home together. I met Penny, who is originally from England, whilst studying in France at university. After graduating we settled in Belfast as it is, by some distance, the best city in the world - at least according to anyone who comes from there. We finished post-graduate study, landed great jobs and were fully involved in our local church. Life was good. After a few years we wanted to start a family. Despite our best efforts we were unable to conceive and after a couple of really difficult years sought medical help. I remember sitting in the home of our consultant physician as he told us that they had uncovered medical issues that we had been unaware of. From that moment we were labelled as "medically infertile": our world came crashing down. Month after month we had to process our disappointment, we had to try to remain positive and believe that it would all turn around, yet here we were being confronted with the news that we may never have a family of our own.

These are typical of the moments that many of us face: it is when what we are confronted with stands in bold opposition to what we have heard about Jesus and His heart for us.

Our circumstances, big and small, can undermine the very notion that Jesus is truly loving, faithful, consistent and the giver of all that is good: the issue is not the circumstances in themselves, but rather how we choose to respond. It is in these moments that I believe that Jesus asks us a question that He first asked His disciples. It is both simple and deeply profound. It strikes to the very core of who we are and what we are building our lives on. How we answer this question will determine our experience of His grace in our lives:

"Who do you say I am?"

How do you answer that? Who do you say Jesus is? A quick Sunday school answer will not suffice when we face tough challenges. In nearly 30 years of ministry, including planting and leading our church here in Belfast, I have seen many people miss out on the life that God had for them as they were overcome by situations that destroyed their faith. I have also seen many more walk into new levels of love, healing, favour and wholeness. This is not because they are better than you or me or because they worked harder and certainly not because they have a special dispensation granted only to the few. It's because they dared to believe that the Jesus revealed to us in the gospels is the same Jesus that lives in us today. Instead of asking "Where is God?" in our troubles, we should be asking "Who is He?" Unlike us, there is no inconsistency with God: He is not chaotic or disordered. How He acts towards us is always perfectly aligned with who He has revealed Himself to be: always good, loving and faithful: the embodiment of grace itself.

After years of doing our best to 'work for' and please God, when confronted with this impossible situation we had nothing to offer! As we wrestled with our disappointment we heard Him gently whisper "Who do you say I am?" It started a journey in us as a couple. We began to sense that our life would be forever different as we opened our hearts to grace.

We had to discover who He really was or truthfully we may have just given up: admittedly it was a long road but today we are blessed with three great kids who were all naturally conceived without the need for medical treatment or intervention!

I want to help you to see your life through the lens of the finished work of Jesus - His unmerited, unearned and undeserved favour.

Each chapter in this book revolves around a story involving Jesus taken from the Gospel of John. Why this gospel in particular? It is different from the others: It was written to show us who Jesus is. Each story or portrait, has a practical application for what we believe about Jesus and how that shapes how we live. This is not a history book or an academic study, but rather an encouragement to embrace a fuller revelation of Jesus in three important ways - who He is, what He has done, and who you are in the light of that.

A key verse in this journey is John 20:31 - *"But these are written that you may believe that Jesus is the Messiah, the Son of God, and that by believing you may have life in His name..."*

I pray that you will grow in faith as you discover the same Jesus in your everyday that we see revealed through these stories. He has not changed: He is still the same and as our hearts become convinced of that truth we will have faith for these days that we live in. This is not about building a life through self effort or performance, but rather a journey where your heart is filled with the goodness and the love of God. He promises that as this happens you will have life in His name. As you read, open your heart and not just your head. Ask Jesus to show you again the scale of His love for you: You will never be the same again.

2

Putting first things first

"But these are written that you may believe that Jesus is the Messiah, the Son of God, and that by believing you may have life in His name."
John 20:31

I never really liked school, I managed to survive it and get through each stage but I have never understood people who loved it. I used to say that there was something wrong with people who enjoyed it! I always felt claustrophobic and spent most of my time thinking about what I would do when I was not locked up behind the school walls. Penny, on the other hand, is one of those people who was totally committed to studying. When we met at university I had to quickly pretend to work more so that she would not write me off entirely. I realised that this was a woman who studied hard and she became the best thing to ever happen to my grades, I was like a different man entirely!

We now live beside an infant school where kids aged four and over begin their formal education. On the first day of term this year I was walking past the school fence when I saw a little boy racing across the playground and heading out towards the gate, he had clearly only managed to make it through three minutes of his first day of the new term before deciding it was not for him. Now carrying his coat and lunchbox he was sprinting for all he was worth in a bid for freedom, his eyes were on the prize and he was not looking back. A teacher was in hot pursuit. She was some way behind him and as I watched him gallop I found myself willing him on - "Run! Run! It only gets worse from here...." I shouted (in my head, not out loud!). I think I could identify with him and how I too felt about being locked up for six hours a day. Despite his best efforts the teacher managed to cut off the escape route and escorted him back to the classroom. Poor kid.

I reflected on this little boy's bid for freedom and it struck me as a metaphor for what we do every day. We are hard wired for freedom in every sense - physical, emotional and spiritual. In our need for wholeness we run towards those things that we believe will make us free. We make choices and build our lives around those things that we think will deliver what we need: we crave peace, health, security, provision, and there is nothing wrong with any of those desires. We yearn for certainty and safety for ourselves and our children however the world we live in is more insecure than ever. There is no shortage of products being marketed by a myriad of companies and organisations promising us that they hold the key to all we hope for. Truthfully a lot of what we try to build on promises much but in the end fails to deliver: Our context in the world today therefore is volatile, uncertain, complex and ambiguous. This is causing anxiety and fear in levels that have been unprecedented in all of history, and Christians are not exempt.

Change the lens

I have been spending some time with my teenage son learning how to fly drones. Whilst I am happy to simply get the drone up and down

Ben operates on a totally different level. He loves to change the camera settings and capture different moods and effects whilst looking at the same landscape that I am looking at. A different lens transforms the experience and what he can see. A few simple tweaks and he captures something quite beautiful that he can take with him after we are done. I am still stuck on the same lens that I started with and that limits my perspective and experience. I tend to see things the same way no matter where we are. Your lens matters. It shapes what you see and how you experience life. How do you navigate through the challenges? Do you fall back onto your own resources and ability or what is your default? As the world gets darker it should cause us to gravitate towards Jesus.

Seeing the same world, circumstances and challenges through the lens of the finished work of grace will lead to your world being transformed. It will cause faith to rise in you and hope to be your song. The biblical word for hope means "to have a confident expectation of good." The Lord promises that, even in these desperately difficult times, His children can expect not just to see the world differently, but to experience it differently as well. Unlike anything else that we could build on, the Bible tells us that the Lord Himself stands watch over His word and promises (Jeremiah 1:12) so that we can put our full faith into who He is.

How do we do that? Let me start by asking you a question.

What are you aligning to? What is your point of reference that you make your decisions from? As you go through each day and are faced by challenges, where does you heart and thinking go to in an attempt to make sense of the situation and find hope for a good outcome? Throughout the COVID pandemic I loved listening to the words of the song Protector. The verse says:

"I come into agreement, With the truth that You are who You say You are, I can trust Your heart. I come into agreement, With what Heaven has declared over my life, Cause I know that You fight for me."
Kim Walker Smith, Album Wild Heart, 2020

What you are aligning to as truth is having a profound effect on your experience of life. We need a deeper revelation of who Jesus is and then we must align our hearts and lives to that truth. We cannot trust ourselves or others to be consistent: we need a bigger perspective that is able to take into account everything that is involved in any situation. We need an external point of reference that lifts our hearts to a place of hope and becomes the lens through which we view our world: from that place wholeness flows. In three out of four gospels it is recorded that Jesus asked His disciples the same question - "Who do you say I am?" He was trying to change their lens. Is He just a prophet? A moral teacher? A heretic? The son of God? He wanted them to see Him for who He truly was and to live from that revelation. He asks the same of you today. Who is Jesus *really* to us?

When Jesus came into the region of Caesarea Philippi, He asked His disciples, saying, "Who do men say that the Son of Man is?" So they said, "Some say John the Baptist, some Elijah, and others Jeremiah or one of the prophets." He said to them, "But who do you say that I am?" Simon Peter answered and said, "You are the Christ, the Son of the living God."
Matthew 16:13-16

Each of us needs to think about how we answer that question for ourselves. In all three gospel accounts (Matthew 16:13-16, Mark 8:27-29 and Luke 9:18-20) Jesus first asks a different question of them. He says:

"Who do the people (crowds) say I am?"

The disciples come up with a whole list of different answers for Jesus:

"Some say John the baptist, others say Elijah; and still others Jeremiah or one of the prophets"
Matthew 16:14

Jesus would often ask questions with a dual purpose - to make people think and to teach them. Many times He would answer a question with another question and in doing so would lead people to think about their situations and find answers. After hearing what the crowds were saying He makes it personal. It is not about what others think or believe. We cannot build our lives solely on someone else's thoughts or opinions. He turns the tables on the disciples and asks - "Who do *you* say I am?" This is key. What the world thinks didn't matter anymore; the mentality of the crowd was irrelevant. We live in a time where a generation is being raised on "likes" - making decisions on what is most "popular" with agendas driven by the crowd. It is increasingly difficult for people to stand for what may be regarded as unpopular beliefs or those that do not fit the new orthodoxy and cultural norms. Even in some corners of the church there is increasing debate about the person and deity of Jesus, with arguments undermining some of the central truths around His life and the events that we read about in scripture. When we are facing tough challenges it really does not matter what Doris from Doncaster on Facebook thinks. There is a time where every one of us, for ourselves, must answer that same question - Who do we say that Jesus is?

In the book *Mere Christianity*, CS Lewis writes:

I am trying here to prevent anyone saying the really foolish thing that people often say about Him: I'm ready to accept Jesus as a great moral teacher, but I don't accept His claim to be God. That is the one thing we must not say. A man who was merely a man and said the sort of things Jesus said would not be a great moral teacher. He would either be a lunatic — on the level with the man who says he is a poached egg — or else He would be the Devil of Hell. You must make your choice. Either this man was, and is, the Son of God, or else a madman or something worse. You can shut Him up for a fool, you can spit at Him and kill Him as a demon or you can fall at His feet and call Him Lord and God, but let us not come with any patronising nonsense about His being a great human teacher. He has not left that open to us. He did not intend to. ... Now it seems to me obvious that He was neither a lunatic nor a fiend: and consequently, however strange or terrifying or unlikely it may seem, I have to accept the view that He was and is God. (ref: Lewis, C. S., Mere Christianity, London: Collins, 1952, pp. 54–56. (In all editions, this is Bk. II, Ch. 3, "The Shocking Alternative.")

Simon Peter, in a moment of divine inspiration, had a revelation about who the church would be built upon:

> *"You are the Messiah, the Son of the Living God"*
> *Matthew 16:16*

It is on this revelation of Jesus that the church; universal and local would be established and would endure: that includes you and me. We all must come to this point for ourselves. Is Jesus just one part of our lives jostling for space alongside everything else; or is He truly the sole point of focus from where we draw the truth of who we are and how we are to live? I believe that in having that same experience as Simon Peter it will catapult us to a transformed way of living with the Lord where we live in a place of increasing promise. This revelation of Jesus as the Messiah, the anointed one is the critical question that is before us today.

Who is the one who saves and delivers us?

Who is the one who heals, restores and brings hope in the challenges and chaos of life? Who are we depending on; is it Jesus alone or someone or something else?

Right back to the beginning

I have seen the goodness of God in many different ways: each day when I look at my own children I am reminded that He is the God of the impossible. I have seen Him provide, protect, encourage and bless my family, and my life. If we were to stop for a moment and reflect it would not be too long before we could come up with a list of the Lord's faithfulness to us. We have seen Him move in our lives yet we desire more of His fullness. When the disciples were having this exchange with Jesus they had already travelled throughout the nation watching Him teach, heal, forgive sins, walk on water, drive out demons and even raise the dead back to life. They had been with Him for some time and had even been sent out in His name to do the same works: yet it is at this point that He asks them "Who do you say I am?" You see we can all live with a level of experience of the Lord's goodness in our lives and still only touch the surface of who He is.

Messiah was often misunderstood in those times, primarily conjuring up the image of a strong military leader who would take by force the freedom that they so desired; the people of Israel yearned for release from the brutality of Roman occupation. We read that the Lord told the disciples not to tell anyone of Peter's confession as they would misunderstand what He had come to do. Jesus came to do so much more than free a group of people from Roman rule: this was not just about outside-in change: it was something altogether more profound.

Jesus was going to show them, and us, that from the very beginning it has always been about His love for us and His work of unmerited favour. He would go to the very core of the human condition by restoring mankind to a place of absolute restoration forever. This was inside-out transformation that goes way beyond only seeing change in outward circumstances.

So let's start on this journey into the Gospel of John and discover again how Jesus revealed Himself as the Messiah.

All of history and prophecy up to this point was expectant for the one who would save. The people were tired and weary; they lived with heavy burdens that were only added to by the religious system of the day. The detail in this gospel is amazing. In the first chapter, after meeting John the Baptist (John 1:19-51), we see different people state who they think Jesus is as they encounter Him. There are seven names, the biblical number of perfection and completion, that reveal to us who Jesus really is. These names are intertwined with situations where Jesus is demonstrating that He is the fulfilment of ancient prophecy about how God would deliver His people. We see in each of these portraits of Jesus a truth about who He is and what that means for us today. The truth found in this gospel will show you that whatever your need, whatever questions you are struggling with in whatever area of your life, Jesus is the answer. Those names that the different people use are: The King of Israel, Rabbi, the Lamb of God, The Son of Man, Jesus of Nazareth, The Son of God and Messiah. If we were to take the whole sense of these names together what would it tell us? Put another way they read:

This fully human Jesus, the Messianic King and teacher of Israel. The Son of God who will die for the sins of the world.

This is the Jesus that I want you to see more clearly than ever before. You will be encouraged as you discover the truth that the Lord does not need you to try harder to succeed, He does not need your performance, He wants your heart: He wants your faith and trust first. As you read remember that grace says "believe" and in believing you will have life. Jesus came not to make you work harder for wholeness but to release you from effort and the demands of the law that you could never live up to anyway. We do not need to try and save ourselves or navigate the complexities of life on our own.

Allow your revelation of Jesus to grow; let His love fill you and you will begin to see transformation of your thinking and experience from the inside out.

3

More than enough

"The Word became human and lived among us."
John 1:14

Sometimes life can be so funny, I love it when I find myself in situations where I am scratching my head at what is going on! I particularly like it when people are very funny without even meaning to be, this happens a lot in Ireland and I believe it is what makes this island such a great place to live. For years before I was in ministry I worked in the world of Corporate Banking and Finance. My role involved dealing with clients and most of the time I was visiting them at their offices and places of work.

One day I was in the south of Ireland heading to a company called Fyffe's who are a major distributor of bananas. At that time my company car was a sporty coupé in racing yellow which I loved, though it divided opinion in the family as to whether I was having a mid-life crisis twenty years too early! I had not visited these offices before so I ended up getting lost and in need of directions: driving down a side street I pulled alongside a man in his sixties who was walking his small dog and seemed to be having a great conversation with it. As I rolled the window down I asked him how I would get to Fyffe's office, looking at me intently he replied in the thickest Irish brogue, "How do ye get 'til there?...Well now that would all depend on where ye are coming from...." With that he just looked at me waiting for my response, I was a little stumped but used my arms to signal that I was in fact coming from, well- here, I mean after all that is where the conversation was taking place!

After about twenty seconds of the most awkward silence known to man he stumped me again. "Do ye work fer Fyffe's?" he asked, puzzled that I may have inadvertently found an Irish prophet I replied that I did not in fact work for them. With a perplexed look on his face he asked "oh ye don't is that right? Then why would ye be driving that?" pointing at my yellow car, at this point I was beaten. To this man it made perfect sense that someone driving a yellow car would work for a banana company. What was probably only about ten seconds felt like an eternity as I sat there without saying a word. I honestly did not know how to respond so I simply thanked him for his help and pulled away slowly, the tears of laughter filling my eyes, making my way down the street I could see the man continuing his conversation with the dog. To this day, every time I see a Fyffe's banana I still chuckle as I think about that conversation and the elderly Irish gentleman who rendered me speechless.

Where are you coming from?

His question is a good one that we should all consider; where are we coming from? Right now you have a construct of Jesus in terms of who He is and what He has done and that is shaping your relationship with Him and the people in your life. It underpins every decision you make and therefore this dictates the course of your life. Hopefully we are on a journey of discovering more about Jesus and living in His truth more each day. I have found that many people live with a hazy view of Jesus shaped through a process of religious osmosis over many years, we have learned to give pat answers to questions about our faith and the person of Jesus.

John in his gospel wants so much more for us, he wants our understanding to grow so that we believe that what is written about Jesus is true; above all other truths and from that place we will then experience 'full life' (John 20:31).

So where are you starting from? If I asked you to take a piece of paper and begin to lay out who Jesus is to you what would that look like? John is often called "The Revelator" because among other things, he unveiled the true identity of Jesus in greater depth than any other biblical author. He drew closer to Jesus than any other disciple and was therefore positioned to have deeper insight into the divine nature of Jesus. It is interesting that John does not begin his gospel with the birth of Jesus like Matthew and Luke, in fact he does not mention the nativity story at all. Instead to help us figure out where we are coming from and where we need to go, he goes right back to the very beginning:

"In the beginning was the Word, and the Word was with God, and the Word was God."
John 1:1

John reveals the deity of Jesus in the very first verse of his gospel. Jesus did not simply become the Son of God when He was born 2000 years ago; He has always been the eternal, pre-existent Son of God: John tells us that He merely assumed a human body in Mary's womb:

18

"The Word became flesh and dwelt among us"
John 1:14

Matthew traces Jesus' ancestry back to Abraham (Matthew 1:1), Luke traces it back to Adam (Luke 3:38) but John goes further and traces it back to God the Father in eternity past. He then goes even further by explaining that Jesus predates time and creation, He was in fact co-creator with His Father:

"He was in the beginning with God. All things were made through Him, and without Him nothing was made that was made."
John 1:2-3

John is setting the scene for you and me, Jesus is not just any other god: He is the eternal and pre-existent God. In Him the whole universe is held together and wherever you are starting from now as you read this, John is suggesting that we get right back to the beginning; that is our baseline. The revelation of Jesus from that starting point helps us to see each of these portraits revealing truth to us in all of their power.

I AM - Your whole life is covered

Over one third of this gospel covers the last week of Jesus' life. In the chapters leading up to that point there are different statements Jesus makes about Himself that will transform how we see Him. Used 735 times in the Bible, the number seven symbolises divine completeness and perfection in both a physical and spiritual sense. Many theologians consider seven to be a holy number, some even saying it's the number of God. Seven derives much of it's meaning from being tied directly to creation. These statements are not a random collection of stories that have just been thrown together, this is Jesus saying that whatever your need is today, the final word is found in His finished work of grace for you. Whatever your question and need may be, the answer is Jesus. These "I am statements" are faith builders for the world that we live in today. In your search for security, hope, and peace the Lord is saying that you do not need to look any further than Jesus and His grace as revealed in these statements. They are more than just writing on a page, they are the truth that He wants to impact your heart with so you can be transformed by His grace. We will look at them in more detail but they are:

- I am the bread of life (John 6:35)
- I am the light of the world (John 8:12)
- Before Abraham was, I AM (John 8:58)
- I am the good shepherd (John 10:11)
- I am the resurrection and the life (John 11:25)
- I am the way, the truth and the life (John 14:6)
- I am the true vine (John 15:1,5)

If you have ever struggled to read your Bible as a complete story then this is going to help you to draw the lines between parts of the Bible that may appear to be completely disconnected. Some people have found that large parts of the Old Testament in particular are just too difficult to make sense of, never mind how they might apply to our lives. As a result we live with many unanswered questions that quietly gnaw away at our faith: The whole biblical narrative is the redemptive story of Jesus; when we see how it all fits together deeper faith comes as a result.

There is a direct connection between Jehovah, I AM, of the Old Testament and Jesus, I AM, in the New Testament. Let's start by examining the first time Moses asked God what His name was at the burning bush:

"God said to Moses I am who I am. Thus you shall say to the children of
Israel I AM has sent me to you."
Exodus 3:14

I AM means the self existent one, the eternal one and is descriptive of the consistent and unchanging nature of God's character. He transcends your past, your present and your future. He has always been and He always will be God. That is great news for us and the challenges that we are individually and collectively facing, there is nothing that we face today that is more powerful than Jesus. So you can fill in the blank right now for your own life: whatever you need from God, it is found in Jesus.

Careful now...

One of the peculiar traits of people from Ireland is our ability not to get too excited: we have become excellent at "not getting ahead of ourselves" which loosely translated means to not think too big or entertain ideas that may sound too fanciful. Whether that is about ourselves or others the principle holds true. It is okay to believe for some goodness in your life as long as you don't get carried away with it. Amazingly this kind of thinking has permeated faith as much as any other part of our society. The result is that we struggle to really see and believe Jesus fully because if we dare to "overstate" the depth of the Lord's goodness, it often clashes with our existing mental frameworks. We have become world leaders at a form of religion that tells people not to have "too much" faith or believe for too much in relation to whatever the issue may be. Why is that? The thinking sounds like this – if things don't work out then people will only be disappointed and that is too difficult to deal with. Therefore our picture of Jesus is often built around limitation and careful expectation management as opposed to the scandalous nature of God's grace and faith to believe that He is the God of breakthrough.

What comes first then?

We need to align our hearts and minds to a new revelation of Jesus. It is not surprising that we see in Jesus' first public miracle a basic pattern that emerges that will repeat through the gospel. John calls the turning of water into wine the first "sign:" it is there to reveal something to us. The pattern goes something like this - Jesus says or does something that reveals another part of who He truly is. He then encourages you and I to make a decision based on what we see. In this case he gets six large ceremonial jars and fills them with water. The jars held around 630 litres of liquid and they were used by people when cleansing themselves under the requirements of the religious law. When the wine initially runs out Jesus turns the water into the highest quality wine, thus saving the hosts from social disaster and shame whilst allowing the party to continue at full speed! After Jesus intervened there was no chance that the party was going to be a flop, He produced 840 bottles of fine wine. There was a certain extravagance to what He did, both in terms of quantity and quality but it was done with clear purpose. There are many layers to this miracle but I want to focus on what it would have meant to the people of that day. The context helps us to draw out richness and meaning that we might otherwise miss: What does this miracle at Cana tell us about Jesus and the kingdom He was bringing?

More than enough

Let's remember that Jesus is drawing the lines from the beginning of time as is written in the Torah, the prophets and the entire biblical narrative to help people understand who He is. The Jews had a long held belief concerning the kingdom of the Messiah and what it would be like in its nature:

"On this mountain the Lord of hosts will make for all peoples a feast of rich food, a feast of well-aged wine, of rich food full of marrow, of aged wine well refined."
Isaiah 25:6

Wine is representative of the covenant blessings God promised to Israel for their obedience and withheld for any disobedience. Wine also represents joy, celebration and festivity; expressing the abundant blessing of God. They believed that a sign of the Messiah's coming kingdom is it would be marked by abundant blessing - both spiritual and physical. Jesus would later use wine as a picture of His blood that would be shed in His crucifixion with the result being that all of us would be set free from sin and death. The point here is that there is a lot of wine produced - and the result is life, celebration, joy and freedom. These are the hallmarks of the Messiah's kingdom.

This matters to us because many of us have bought into the original lie that deceived Adam and Eve in the garden of Eden. The ultimate lie was that God was holding back from us and that we did not have everything needed to flourish fully. Therefore when the enemy suggested that Eve eat the forbidden fruit from the tree of the knowledge of good and evil, she did so because she felt that she had needs that were not being fulfilled by God. She did not see provision, she saw lack, often called a scarcity mindset. It is the thinking that says that God is not enough. He may be able to meet some of your needs but even if He is able to meet all of them, you cannot guarantee that He will. Too often we focus on what we do not have instead of recognising what has been given to us through grace. What happens when we live from a distrustful, scarcity mindset? The answer is that we begin to justify selfish, self-centered behaviour. This has always been the same and we see it in so many Bible characters: the violence of Cain in Genesis 4, Abraham's deception in Genesis 12 or Jacob's lies are all rooted in a lack and scarcity mindset. In the Old Testament we see that every time the people of Israel live in this way, it leads them on a course of destruction.

God's response to our history of selfishness is not to condemn us but in a reversal of expectations He decides to give you and I the ultimate gift - His very own Son:

"For the law was given through Moses; Grace and truth came through Jesus Christ."
John 1:17

We act selfishly because our revelation of Jesus is too small: when we do not see that every need is met in His work of grace then our only option is to take responsibility on our own shoulders. This is where we fall from grace and back to the demands of a performance faith that results in a cycle of defeat and failure. Another layer in the story of Cana perfectly illustrates the difference between living in law and that of receiving grace. In Exodus 7 we read the story of the first public miracle of Moses. In response to the hardness of Pharaoh, Moses turns the river Nile into blood and many people die. When we contrast that with Cana we see that the new covenant of grace is much different. Jesus turns the water to wine (remember enough to fill about 840 normal wine bottles!) and it is not death that follows but life and celebration: He supplied way more than what was needed.

The point is that no matter what your capacity is for effort and self-sufficiency, it will never produce in you what one touch of His grace will do in a moment. Jesus sets the scene for us and challenges our selfishness and expands our view of what His kingdom is all about. He wants us to see that He is abundant, plentiful and generous. His blessing and grace will never run out, we will never exhaust the depth of His love and provision. When He moves on our behalf He will over-supply where we have need. He is not the God of lack or 'just enough.' Whatever you are facing today be encouraged that He is well able to provide for you in every area of your life. You are not called to carry the weight and responsibility of provision for health, finance, future, family and every other pressure life throws at us. He is the abounding, generous King and His kingdom reflects His nature. That is what Jesus announced at Cana; that is great news for those of us in need today.

4

Heaven is here

"My dwelling place shall be with them"
Ezekiel 37:27

I often find myself walking through the centre of Belfast, the city where I was born and now live with my family. If you were to visit today with no prior knowledge of the city's history, you would agree that it is a fantastic place to explore. A place with such a rich history, including being the birthplace of icons such as the Titanic and many other innovations that took over the world. I'm not sure why we are so proud of building a ship that sank on its first big trip, that is still something of a mystery yet we are very proud of it! If you ask any local they will be quick to tell you that it was fine when it left here! Belfast has produced many world leaders in the arts, music, industry, innovation and has become a home for many of the world's leading digital companies.

However it is also a deeply divided city: for nearly 30 years, starting in the late sixties, a conflict known as "The Troubles" raged throughout Northern Ireland. Division along religious, cultural and nationalist lines led to the deaths of 3,500 people and left many tens of thousands more physically injured and mentally scarred. To this day deep division and fracture remains. I grew up through the 1980's and early 1990's and I vividly remember some of the worst atrocities of the troubles as though they were yesterday, it affected everyone who lived here. Often the random nature of gun and bomb attacks meant that people were afraid to socialise and go out, life was certainly far from any accepted definition of normal. The job that my own Dad did made him a target for those from the "other side" and I can remember many nights as a young boy feeling petrified as he went out to work, wondering if he would return safe.

It was at the very height of the troubles that my parents started to go to church and came to faith. Nearly everyone in Northern Ireland at that stage had a history with a church, whether Catholic or Protestant, it is a very religious country. Even though my parents did not attend church when I was young, they still sent my brother and I out every week to Sunday School where we would be entertained by some wonderful people who were incredibly faithful in looking after us. At that time a new church movement linked to the Charismatic renewal was being established around Belfast and we started going there as a family.

Why am I telling you this? I can remember that church quickly became a huge anchor and place of safety in my life, I loved it - every bit of it. Each week we would go and although now I cannot remember most of what happened in detail I have never forgotten how it made me feel as a young kid who was growing up surrounded by so much destruction and hatred in our city. I don't think for one minute that I was any different to most kids growing up through the troubles but I started to understand that even in the physical space of church, I would feel safe. I felt like I belonged there and I loved just even being in the building. I spent as much time as I could getting involved in nearly every ministry of the church. In fact it was the only place that I was "grounded" from when I was a teenager: that means my Dad banned me from going to church-just think about that. Looking back on that episode with my Dad I did ask him what on earth he was thinking at the time in stopping my church privileges. It is hardly typical teenage rebellion and to this day I'm still not sure we have a good answer to what he was thinking, he just chuckles to himself when we talk about it.

Heaven meets earth

Where do you go to feel safe and protected? This is a deep need in the post-COVID world, where are we safe? As we look at these portraits of Jesus we see that He takes many of the normal things in their world and shows that they pointed to who He is. John 2 and 3 take place with Passover as the background context. Jesus takes two of the most important things to the Jews and shows them that they were about Him: the first part of our story happens in a place of massive national, cultural and religious significance - the temple.

In the Bible there are two temples mentioned. The first temple was built by King David's son Solomon and was destroyed by the Babylonians in 576 BC. The second temple was built by Zerubbabel and was destroyed by the Romans in AD 70.

It is in this second temple that we read the story of Jesus clearing the traders who were selling oxen, sheep and pigeons that were used in the sacrifices. The money changers also received a harsh rebuke by Jesus as He rallied against those who had made the temple into a place of exploitation and profit when it was supposed to be so much more. At the end of this event we read some words that left the religious people really stumped:

The Jews said to him, "What sign do you show us for doing these things?" Jesus answered them, "Destroy this temple, and in three days I will raise it up." The Jews then said, "It has taken forty-six years to build this temple, and will you raise it up in three days?" But he was speaking about the temple of his body.
John 2:18-21

The religious people did not get what He was talking about. What is all this talk of building temples in three days? What was Jesus showing you and I in this and why would it even matter to us today? If we look at the perspective of a Jewish person from that time, God had given them two very clear instructions about where He would be present on the earth:

"And let them make me a sanctuary, that I may dwell in their midst."
Exodus 25:8-9

"I will make a covenant of peace with them. It shall be an everlasting covenant with them. And I will set them in their land and multiply them, and will set my sanctuary in their midst forevermore. My dwelling place shall be with them."
Ezekiel 37:26-27

This physical temple was the place where God said He would be with them: it housed the very presence of God Almighty and they depended on that for blessing and protection. They knew that if the presence of God was with them then the nation would be safe and successful: that is why the temple was of such importance, it was the very place where heaven meets earth; the point where they touch. It is here that the fullness of the presence and power of God would be established in the world. There was one big problem though – the ordinary people could not go into that place where the presence of God was found: it was hidden behind a curtain and death was the result if they went into the holiest place. The temple for the ordinary person was the place where they had to go and pay the price for their sins. They brought offering after offering in a never ending cycle of payment for their mess, hoping that they would find forgiveness and favour with God. They were kept on the outside and could never know what it meant to connect with God in His very presence: there was no way in for the ordinary man or woman.

The temple that Jesus cleared was also seen by the religious ruling classes to be the centre of absolute truth where the law was debated and the religious rules were made. We are told that the Sanhedrin, a judicial council headed by the High Priest, met in the temple in the Hall of Hewn Stones. It would eventually be Caiaphas and the Sanhedrin that condemned Jesus for blasphemy, leading to His crucifixion. The law was hard on the people and burdened ordinary men and women with demands that they could not meet, no matter how hard they tried. It had become a place of demand, penalty and obligation; not a place of blessing, life, and connection with their creator.

There's more to it

Do you ever feel that there must be something more for you than what you are seeing right now? Have you experienced that longing? This is what it was like for the Jews in this story from John 2. In this temple exchange Jesus is opening their eyes and ours eyes to a truth that they had been taught for generations but had just not understood the reason why it was so significant. In Ezekiel 47 we read about a prophet who had lived for 25 years with the failure of his nation Israel. Yet the Lord shows Him where the great sweep of salvation will begin, it will start a movement that will change human beings for eternity. He has a vision of the life and grace of God changing everything that it touches, he sees a river of life that will overcome even death itself.

Then he brought me back to the entrance of the temple; there, water was flowing from below the threshold of the temple towards the east (for the temple faced east); and the water was flowing down from below the south end of the threshold of the temple, south of the altar. Then he brought me out by way of the north gate and led me round on the outside to the outer gate that faces towards the east; and the water was coming out on the south side.
Ezekiel 47:1-2

Wherever the river goes, every living creature that swarms will live, and there will be very many fish, once these waters reach there. It will become fresh; and everything will live where the river goes.
Ezekiel 47:9-10

This is a vision of a river of life that flows out from the temple and everything that it touches turns from death to life. This is a prophecy of the coming Messiah and what His ministry would be like: the Messiah would come not to live in a building made of brick and stone. God would walk among us, be made flesh. The new temple would not be made from stone but would be the body of Jesus Himself, He would give this body up in a final sacrifice for all mankind. The river of His life, the Holy Spirit, now flows bringing healing, feeding, nourishing, bearing fruit and providing fulfilment to a desolate land and a people in dire need. This is what the temple was supposed to be - the place where heaven meets earth! From there the fullness and beauty of heaven is poured out onto everything that touches it.

31

Jesus is saying that the physical building was only supposed to be a sign of something so much greater - Jesus Himself. His body was heaven wrapped up in human form and He was the one that had come now to earth. The fullness of heaven was colliding with their world. No longer would ordinary people like you and me be caught in a system of heavy condemnation and performance that could never really transform us out of sin. Never again would a religious system designed by men be allowed to keep the ones that God so loves out of His presence. The temple was a reminder that, although there is pain and mess all around us, there is an Eden, (scenes from Eden were carved into the wood in the temple) where we can be fully connected with God without anything getting in the way. The whole of heaven wrapped up in human form and now here on earth for everyone.

Jesus announced that if we want to experience new life then it would be found in Him and not in any building: the people did not understand that and sometimes I do not think that we do either. Everything that you and I need will never be found in service, ministry, education, performance or whatever else we may give ourselves to. It is not that any of these things are intrinsically bad, Jesus is telling us that He is the only place where we can experience heaven on earth, in His presence. The places where His grace and His favour touch become fruitful and full of life. He shows us that life flows from Him and where there are dead places in our lives we need to bring those under His grace and allow His life to transform us from the inside out.

Through the window

If you have been around church for any length of time you will know that there are verses that we have heard that are used to get something out of people, whether it be money, time or service. Money is a great example and I have heard many preachers bash people over the heads with scriptures taken so clearly out of the context in which they were written. What would heaven on earth look like in your life right now? Are you sick or do you have a loved one that is suffering right now? Perhaps you struggle with anxiety and mental health issues that no one has been able to find breakthrough in? Do you find yourself in a battle for your own self worth, constantly comparing yourself to others and feeling like you never measure up? Or perhaps you worry about provision and financial security.

There are endless opportunities for things to occupy our hearts and rob us of our peace. Imagine for one moment how those situations would look different if they received even one touch of this river of grace that flows from Jesus, that is what He came for. Malachi 3 has often been misinterpreted in the area of giving to leave many Christians struggling under the weight of fear and condemnation. The truth is that it is a clear picture of what it means to have heaven meet earth.

Let me explain a little of the background here that will help this come alive. Unlike in the West, letters of the Hebrew alphabet are also used for numbers and they have a picture associated with them. The fifth letter is "hei-[ה]" and in ancient Hebrew this letter is a window, meaning that it reveals something. Think about it, a window illuminates and permits the light to shine through so that nothing is hidden. Rabbis agree that this is indeed what the fifth letter is but they do not know what it reveals. Under the law we will never see grace:

"open the windows of heaven for you and pour down for you a blessing until there is no more need"
Malachi 3:10

We also know that five is the number of grace; remember grace means the unearned, undeserved and unmerited favour of God. There is no way that you and I could ever do anything in and of ourselves that would qualify us for the life of heaven in every area of our lives, not a chance. Here we see what it means when heaven meets your world, what happens when your mess or pain collides with His grace? If you want to imagine that then you have to see through the open window of grace to the fullness of the blessing that the Lord promises. You cannot see through the lens of your own effort and performance as that will never be enough. The verse then says that through grace you will receive all *until you have no more need.* That is the abundance of the kingdom that Jesus announced at Cana. It is not just about the Lord scraping you through each day but allowing you to experience the blessing of heaven through His grace until you have no more need. That is good news for you today. Heaven touching earth is not about rules, regulations and burden but rather about us experiencing the life of heaven that meets the demand of all that we face.

What will you make of this truth today? When Jesus was crucified the final curtain literally fell in the temple: the days of separation were over. The huge curtain that kept the ordinary man and woman from experiencing heaven and the presence and power of God was ripped from top to bottom. The meaning is clear, the promise of personal connection to God and the ability to receive all that you need from Him was made available forever. When Jesus died God moved out of that place and said that He would never again dwell in a temple made by human hands. He was finished with that religious system and the restrictions that it put on His people. Jesus prophesied (Luke 13:35) that the temple would be destroyed and it was by the Romans in AD 70.

Let me finish this by circling back on where we started. I have always loved the house of God. When I was that kid growing up I did think that it was because there was something special about the building and the place. Actually what I was encountering was not about the bricks and the mortar. My inside world was receiving grace. It was heaven touching my world and although I could not articulate it I certainly could feel the difference. The Lord wants us to keep growing in this revelation. Our local church families are critical for our spiritual walk. We were never designed to do life alone. We are to be found not just in a physical space but together in the presence of Jesus. He challenges our small thinking by telling us that He is an abundant, generous King and His kingdom that we are called into is marked by life and celebration. This life is a picture of heaven that is available to all people everywhere, at any time. You and I can experience heaven on earth individually and together. Heaven meeting earth as His grace is poured out into our lives, transforming every situation.

5

New heart, new spirit

*"unless one is born of **water and the Spirit,** he cannot enter the kingdom of God."*
John 3:5

I used to love Wednesday evenings when I was a young kid. We lived on a housing estate where I attended the local primary school with my older brother. In my P6 year (age 9/10) my school teacher invited us to a midweek children's meeting at a local church that she attended. Every Wednesday evening she would drive an old bus around the estate, picking up groups of kids to bring them to church. We would arrive half gassed on the petrol fumes that filled the cabin of the bus, Health and safety was not as finely honed back then as it is today! On arrival we would run in and sit on benches to listen to stories of the Bible that were told through the medium of Fuzzy Felt.

We heard it all - the great heroes of our faith and their exploits for God, stories about Jesus and His disciples, Paul's great missionary journeys and the birth of the church. Towards the end of each night we were given the opportunity to respond to the final presentation. Looking back I am surprised that we did not suffer from nightmares as this part of the evening was the *Fuzzy Felt Hell Edition* presented by an elderly man with a puppet. For a long period of time it felt as though we were dangled over the pit of hell itself to the point where I could feel the flames licking around my ankles, if we had done anything wrong since the last time we repented, then we had to get saved all over again just to be sure that we were not in danger of eternal damnation. I mean what would happen if Jesus were to come back that night?

I can remember that puppet as clearly today and the fear that it struck into us. Every week without fail I would put my hand up in recognition that I had tipped the scales towards wrath and judgment. I would respond with nearly all the other kids in the hope that Jesus would not be quick to send me to hell when he realised just how bad I was. Please hear me, I am in no way criticising those people who served the kids of our estate through the pretty bleak times of the troubles, I am grateful for their heart and commitment to bring us to faith and to spend their time and money in that pursuit. In all weathers they pursued us and created the best opportunity that they knew of to help us encounter God. With the benefit of experience, personal encounter and testimony I do have a different perspective on the character and nature of the Lord, but I will be forever grateful for their commitment to reaching me.

Does God trust me?

This is at the heart of the next portrait and it is one that really gets to a root that is common to all of us, no matter who you are or where you come from. After Cana and the temple we read that the message of Jesus is starting to gain some traction with the people:

Now when He was in Jerusalem at the Passover Feast, many believed in his

name when they saw the signs that he was doing. But Jesus on his part did
not entrust himself to them, because he knew all people"
John 2:23-24

These verses at the very end of Chapter 2 give a false division in the narrative that we are reading. John did not neatly cut his work into the chapters that we have today. The very next line in Chapter 3 verse 1 is supposed to be read in the context of the verses above:

"There was a man..."
John 3:1

Although people were putting their faith in Jesus, He would not trust Himself to them in response. Why? Because He knows how fickle and frail we all are. The scene is being set for us, Jesus says He understands what is in the heart of men and then immediately John sets us up to meet a man who is a key figure in the Jewish nation. In fact this man is the senior teacher of the law who carries the title "The Teacher of Israel". There is something in this exchange that we must pay attention to, the Lord wants us to see this teacher's issue is also ours. John is not belittling the teacher as an individual but rather it is written to help understand our own issue more clearly. We should approach this encounter with an openness to be transformed by grace as we watch what unfolds when the teacher meets Jesus.

We are talking of course about Nicodemus - the Teacher of Israel. He represents man's best efforts to get right with God through personal effort and law keeping, he is at the pinnacle of those who teach the Torah and knows the intricacies of the law better than anyone else. Whilst to human ears that may sound impressive but that kind of approach is not something that Jesus trusts; here is the person that represents the pinnacle of human understanding in respect of what the law demands and what right living before God looks like. Yet Jesus does not trust that way of living or that manner of approaching Him.

An awkward conversation

We all know what it is like to be in a really awkward conversation. I have been in many situations where I just wanted the rapture to happen in that moment so I could be whisked away from the embarrassment of it all. Nicodemus in his lofty position would also have been a skilled political operator. He was adept at working with people and managing relationships that were required to keep him in position, he was savvy and streetwise. He heard about the miracles that Jesus was performing and the growing support among the people for this man from Nazareth. He approaches Jesus in the manner that was normal to him by trying to win him over through flattery:

> *"No one can do these signs unless God is with them."*
> *John 3:2*

Watch how Jesus handles this, it's a masterclass at getting to the heart of the issue. He cuts through the manoeuvering and refuses to play games; He is no different with you and me. He does not play games with us or fix our issues by playing around the edges of our lives. His love does a profound work in us. In fact He promised that this love would do the deepest work of transformation in us. It is not an outside-in sticking plaster but a total renewal from the inside-out. Jesus replies:

> *"Truly, truly, I say to you, unless one is born again (anōthen) he cannot see (hor-ah'-o, perceive, experience, discern) the kingdom of God."*
> *John 3:3*

39

In my part of the world this expression "born again" has become an expression of disdain for people who take issue with religion and how they perceive it has been detrimental to people and society; however it is a powerful truth that speaks to every human heart. Jesus takes this ardent law keeper and shows Him that He has missed the point entirely. He wants Nicodemus to understand that He is the fulfillment of long established prophecies to the people of Israel that the Messiah would set them free from bondage. The word that Jesus uses here is *anōthen* which has two different meanings. Firstly it can relate to time. Jesus intends another meaning here which is *"from above"* (John 3:32). Nicodemus is slow on the uptake and does not grasp what Jesus is talking about, he takes the first meaning and it leaves him wondering how we are supposed to return to our mother's womb. Jesus needs to help Nicodemus so He comes back to the same point and essentially says the same thing again using a different metaphor. From a cursory glance it seems to add to his, and our confusion:

> Jesus answered, "Truly, truly, I say to you, unless one is born of **water and the Spirit,** he cannot enter the kingdom of God."
> John 3:5

Is Jesus being deliberately vague and difficult here or is He trying to get to something much deeper and more profound? Remember the Gospel of John was written with the purpose of revealing Jesus as the Messiah as described towards the end of the book:

> "But these are written that you may believe that Jesus is the Messiah, the Son of God, and that by believing you may have life in His name."
> John 20:31

The Lord wants you and I to see Jesus as the only true Messiah and in believing that we will have life: so what did He mean?

Who is the boss really?

Why does Jesus use these words and what do they mean for us? On the surface it looks like Jesus is speaking standard new creation type talk. Again if we remember who He is talking to we begin to see the layers that make this much more profound. He is talking to the Teacher of Israel; the image is clear. Nicodemus is a picture of what sits as the authority in your life. Jesus is speaking to the root of our issue, the condemnation that drives our best efforts and law keeping in order to please God. Many of us have become good at knowing how to play the game and say the right thing. Jesus wants to cut through all of that and get to the very heart of the issue. If we hear what He is saying then we will find new levels of freedom and life that would never be possible through our own efforts. This is something bigger than us and what we do through our actions, Nicodemus would have understood that full well. Jesus shows that it was always the heart of God that we would be born spiritually by grace and live in that grace through faith. From the very beginning it was never the heart or intention of God that we would survive through self effort and performance with God added on after we had exhausted all that we can do ourselves.

Let's back up - Jesus is going way back

Jesus is drawing the bigger picture for Nicodemus by going back to the prophet Ezekiel. He shows us that unearned, undeserved, unmerited favour was always God's heart. It is not that grace is an add on, but it is the whole deal, it is not a niche area of theology. In Nicodemus we see that when we mix our own effort with His grace we actually come to a place where we miss the point entirely! When we try to frame our works alongside God's grace it has the effect of negating the work of that grace within us:

"I do not nullify the grace of God; for if justification were through the law,
then Christ died to no purpose"
Galatians 2:21

God's desire for you is that you would lean into and trust wholly in His love and work: from that posture everything flows to us. Ezekiel 36 and 37 are two well known chapters that are a prophetic look at what God would do with His people; Nicodemus would have known these writings inside and out but he could not see that they were being fulfilled right in front of him:

*"I will take you from the nations and gather you from all the countries and bring you into your own land. **I will sprinkle clean water on you, and you shall be clean from all your uncleannesses, and from all your idols I will cleanse you.**"*
Ezekiel 36:24-25

"And I will give you a new heart, and a new spirit I will put within you. And I will remove the heart of stone from your flesh and give you a heart of flesh."
Ezekiel 36:26

"And I will put my Spirit within you, and cause you to walk in my statutes and be careful to obey my rules"
Ezekiel 36:27

When Jesus talks about being born from above and being born of water He's drawing the lines for Nicodemus back to something that he would have read thousands of times. Ezekiel says that there is a day coming where we would be free from every ounce of sin, death, dysfunction and all its' consequences. We would be released from the weight and demands of the law so that we could really experience the life that God has for us. In verse 25 "idols" refer to anything that we put our faith and trust in. Today, many of us have made an idol of our performance for God; We can be more concerned with what we are doing for Him rather than what He has done for us. Our faith is often in what we do and that is what matters most to us.

Why is this important? These verses show us that it is only the gift of God's grace that will free us from sin. God never believed that we would be able to keep ourselves out of sin. Nicodemus and those who kept the law were so bound in fear that they would miss God yet they ended up doing just that. They reduced relationship with God to a complex set of outward focused rituals that did nothing to change their own hearts or those of the people. God does not want that from us. He wants our hearts to be connected to Him in a relationship of love. What's worse is that rule keeping is absolutely powerless to help us love the Lord or walk free from sin. When we receive the gift of forgiveness and no condemnation, the Holy Spirit helps us to choose the life that God has for us. Living connected to God through grace brings life in ways that the rules never will.

When Paul was writing to the church in Corinth he made it clear: the more you try through your own effort, the more you strengthen sin! (1 Corinthians 15:56). Nicodemus was floored by this; everything that he had built his world around was being dismantled right in front of him. Jesus was not trying to embarrass or humiliate him, He was revealing a totally different way of relating to God that would actually result in holiness and right living. That kind of life is a God gift that we simply receive! If you are reading this and are struggling in an area let me encourage you clearly. You do not need less grace, you need more. You do not need more self effort but more grace that produces breakthrough and good fruit.

The aha moment

Penny and I do not watch a lot of television. That is not making some sort of statement about people who do but rather just an observation that with church, family and business, our days are busy and we do not have a lot of time to devote to television. When we do watch something it is usually a series with an engaging story line, I love it when a story unfolds and you start to put the pieces together. Something happens, a character says something or you see a scene that fills in the blanks and there is that "aha" moment, what was foggy starts to become clear. I imagine as Nicodemus listened to Jesus speaking that this is what was happening: the lights were coming on. It was not just his head understanding but it was also his heart filling with the truth, he knew what was coming next as Ezekiel continued his prophecy in Chapter 37:

"Prophesy to these bones and say to them, 'Dry bones, hear the word of the Lord! This is what the Sovereign Lord says to these bones: I will make breath enter you, and you will come to life."
Ezekiel 37:4-5

Jesus says that to have this kind of new life we must be born of the Spirit. God would impart His own breath into dry bones and they would come alive; this would be for all humanity. Put yourself in the place of Nicodemus and it starts making more and more sense. We come to God trying to maintain a standard that dooms us to failure before we even begin! There is no life, just a cycle of defeat where the best seems to escape us. Jesus looks at us and says I never wanted that for you; it was always about me and my work for you, it is never the other way around. Just like when Jesus said He was finished with the system of the temple, He is now referring to the age that was passing away (Hebrews 9:8-9) and a new covenant between us and God that was being established.

I think that Nicodemus was struggling to get this but before we judge him let's remind ourselves that we still find it difficult to truly walk in this truth today; even though we have heard it, we do not truly grasp it. Jesus said, we "marvel" at it. The original word means to be "astonished" or "begin to speculate upon the matter":

> "Do not marvel that I said to you, 'You must be born again.'"
> John 3:7

Like Nicodemus you may even find yourself reacting to this gift of grace: for any number of reasons we can be desperate to add to what Jesus has done for us, we feel the need to make a contribution. It feels like unless we can add to it then it is not worth as much: Jesus is unambiguous. The only way to be remotely acceptable to God, living free from your mess and living blessed, is by being born from above. It is a gift that no system of rule keeping will ever achieve. Towards the end Jesus says some of the most famous verses that are known today:

> Nicodemus said to him, "How can these things be?" Jesus answered him, "Are you the teacher of Israel and yet you do not understand these things?...." "For God so loved the world, that he gave his only Son, that whoever believes in him should not perish but have eternal life. For God did not send his Son into the world to condemn the world, but in order that the world might be saved through him"
> John 3:9-10, 16-17

Jesus didn't come into your world to reinforce, adapt or re-establish a system that would condemn you. The more that you allow yourself to believe that your own effort is moving the dial of God's love for you, the harder it will be for you to see the fullness of His love and grace. Just like it is for us, it was too hard for Nicodemus to grasp. It seems to be too simple and too good to be true. It offends us. Surely I can add my piece? That option is forever closed to us, Grace shows us a better way!

There is a neat progression through these first portraits of Jesus as John paints a picture of showing us who He really is. The image becomes more clear as each line unfolds. He has announced that this kingdom would be abundant, full of life and a cause for celebration. Full of the very best wine. He announces that we can live in the goodness of heaven right now because He is the place where heaven meets earth. Now He shows us that this life that flows from Him will never be experienced because of your effort. You can be made brand new. You do not need to live dry and burdened anymore, you can only receive this renewal as a gift and allow His Spirit to breathe it into you. From there you will start to live in the kind of freedom that was His design from the very beginning. For a world that is desperate for renewal and meaning, this is still amazingly good news today.

6

Total freedom

"Come, see a man who told me all that I ever did."
John 4:29

When I get involved in something I tend to throw my whole self into it, no half measures: 'Go big or go home'. With experience I have found that that can be a good trait, but at times can be less helpful. I also find that it can be hard to be on the outside of something looking in. I don't like to see others excluded and so I try my best to make sure that everyone who wants to be involved can be, in whatever is happening. When I was a younger teenager our youth group was involved in a huge missions event in Belgium called "Love Europe." Organised by Operation Mobilisation, it involved thousands of young people coming from all over Europe to Belgium and Holland for weeks of teaching and street evangelism.

In all honesty that was not the main reason for me being so excited about this trip, it should have been all about the mission but I was one of the youngest in the group and I just loved hanging out with my friends. Thinking about it now, I would rather have my teeth pulled by an amateur dentist than driving from Belfast to Belgium in a packed minibus, for three weeks of living in a tent with a load of strangers. At the time though I could think of nothing better. The sense of adventure, the experience of new cultures, freedom from my parents, the laughs and the memories that would be made, this was going to be the trip of a lifetime. That is until my youth group leader took me to the side and told me that I was not old enough to go, I didn't meet the age threshold and I was the only one that would be unable to travel.

I was devastated when I heard the news. What made it worse was that I still had to help everybody else raise funds and listen as the team would talk about all the laughs they were going to have, talk about rubbing salt in the wound! When they all left it was the first time in my life that I had genuinely felt on the outside, and I did not like it. This was nobody's fault and yet I was gutted. Even though it was not personal, it felt like it was. To try and take my mind off it my parents took me to our favourite place in the Mourne mountains. My mum tells me that I spent the whole time asking what the others would be doing at that exact moment, I think I drove them all to distraction.

Made for belonging

We were made to belong, we were not made to be on the outside; this is an intrinsic need in the make up of all of us. It is the God given part of us that needs to connect with Him first and discover who we are from there. That's why we see in these first chapters of John, Jesus taking the every day institutions, such as marriage, the temple and religion and revealing that He was the reality and fulfilment to which they all pointed. In this next scene we see Jesus taking another key foundation of life at the time and showing how it illustrated who He is.

Whilst traveling with the disciples Jesus came to a town in Samaria called

Sychar, near the field that Jacob had given to his son Joseph. There are so many layers to this story it would take a whole book to capture them all. Jesus had gone out of His way to travel here, this was not a place that Jews would normally visit. Even today He goes out of His way so that He can reach you wherever you are. Jesus arrives at Jacob's well and being tired from his journey he sits down beside it, it was about the middle of the day. A woman from Samaria came to draw water and Jesus said to her:

"Give me a drink."
John 4:5-7

Jesus has taken a detour to a place where the disciples really did not want to be so that they could encounter a woman at a well. This is an ancient story that speaks clearly to the multitude of issues that we are facing in the 21st century. It is one of the clearest examples of how Jesus looks at those whom He loves and so it is deeply encouraging for us today. It is difficult to describe why this interaction is so controversial. To start this is a Jewish rabbi speaking to a Samaritan woman on his own, and not just any woman, a woman with a really colourful back story. First let's look at where this all happens.

The well

The context for these interactions brings new depth to what we read, throughout the Bible wells were very significant places. In a land that was dry and parched they sustained life for families and entire communities . Without a source of water it was impossible to survive. A well therefore was not a luxury, but rather essential to existence. They were often given meaningful names that had strong spiritual connotations. Many notable events happen at different wells throughout the Bible, for example the revelation of God to Hagar (Genesis 16). Normally when people came to an unoccupied piece of land they would dig a well and this would become a lifeline for the community and a landmark for weary travellers. Due to the topography of the land these wells were often very deep, going down far into the earth. The one in this story was called Jacob's well (Genesis 29) and is found today near modern day Nablus in Israel. So the scene is set: wells are all about water and the fact that we need water to live. Quite simply, if there is no water, then there is no life. This theme of water is an important thread that John continues following on from the prophecy of Ezekiel that we talked about in the last chapter.

I don't want to go there

How often have you found yourself somewhere and wished that you could be somewhere else? Every single time I visit a dentist I would trade that moment for anything that you asked. I think it is rooted in my childhood when our family dentist was affectionately called 'psycho'. To this day I am not sure if he had ever heard the word gentle, or he was just working out his deep issues on each patient, either way it put me off dentists and that has never changed. The disciples here were in a similar position, they thought that they were headed for Galilee yet they found themselves in enemy territory. They would not have chosen to pass through here, let alone visit, but Jesus had other ideas, there are so many layers to this story that bring us encouragement. Recently we have been through a period in world history that nobody saw coming and frankly nobody would have chosen. The COVID-19 pandemic caused death and disruption on a global scale, bringing with it a large amount of uncertainty and fear about the future. Like the disciples we found ourselves in a place that we did not plan for and did not want. The Lord though is not limited by or bound to what it happening in the natural world; this story shows that He always has a bigger purpose and no matter where you are He will cause you to thrive:

"Look, lift up your eyes and see, already...."
John 4:35

Jesus tells His disciples that the power and presence of God are available for them and there is no delay or need to wait. They are focused on their natural surroundings and so He tells them to 'look up' and see what He is doing at that moment; they need a shift in perspective. They probably felt like they wanted to be somewhere else, but in reality they needed to see God right where they were; He is always working exactly where we are. Often what is required for us to move from fear to blessing is to lift up our eyes and see with His perspective. There are things in motion in your life right now that are ordained by the Lord. You may not yet be able to see them with your natural eyes, but there are people, circumstances, situations all being worked together for your good: that is not a pipe dream for some time, but a promise for you today! We may think that we disqualify ourselves from His grace, but Jesus demonstrates that no matter who you are, or where you find yourself, you can receive all you need from Him.

Inflammatory or what?

This story speaks right to the heart of the issues that are dominating the world today: race, gender and socio-economic challenges are all touched upon through the character of this woman. Jesus breaks three different traditions to show us something amazing: as we look at each of these we can see that though we may be bound by traditions or the opinions of others, there is nothing that will stop the Lord from breaking into our worlds with His grace.

First He speaks with a woman. As a man and a Jewish rabbi that was unheard of. She is gathering water at the hottest part of the day which shows us that she has been rejected by the people of her village; the women would gather water in the early morning when it was cooler, yet it is clear that she is not welcome in that group: she is on the outside, she is a reject. Her repeated moral failure has left her without friendship or help.

Secondly, we know that she is a Samaritan and they were detested by the Jews. Samaritans were a mixed race who had intermarried with the Assyrians. The Jews refused to live, mingle or worship with them; deep differences in religious thinking separated the groups further. Notice that Jesus is not making a judgment about this woman based on any of those things. He looks past all the usual list of disqualifications, His perspective is totally different.

Finally He takes a drink from her, this simple act would have rendered Him ceremonially unclean. The woman was judged by every single group as an outcast, yet Jesus demonstrates that His grace is stronger than judgment: where she is condemned, His love reaches in! This is a moment of profound healing for the woman and in showing such love and compassion, Jesus shows us how He deals with you and I today. He has not changed. He is still the same.

Interestingly, He does not ever ignore her situation or her condition:

Jesus said to her, "Go, call your husband, and come here." The woman answered him, "I have no husband." Jesus said to her, "You are right in saying, 'I have no husband'; for you have had five husbands, and the one you now have is not your husband. What you have said is true."
John 4:16-18

Jesus never looks past what is going on with us, He is never intimidated by our mess. He lifts our heads up from our brokenness so His love can lead us to freedom: He knows that His grace is more powerful than our past history and current situation. Whilst He is fully aware of this woman's circumstance and her story, He refuses to let it define who she is or what her future could be. There is an important order here: most of us have been conditioned that we are more lovable or acceptable when we get ourselves cleaned up. We are told that our dysfunction causes a relational deficit that must be made up before we are in a position to be loved by God. Jesus does not ask us to change before He loves us. Look at how He treats this woman; before anything else He loves her, honours her, shows her respect and dignity, He does not exclude or judge her based on her failure. The inner legalist in each of us can struggle with that: it's easier to love people when they fit with our view of what "right" looks like. When we treat others that way it shines a spotlight onto how we think God treats us, there is a big lesson here:

"Or do you presume on the riches of His kindness and forbearance and patience, not knowing that God's kindness is meant to lead you to repentance?"
Romans 2:4

The only route to real change in our lives is to first receive His love and grace: I call this the gift of no condemnation. Repentance and transformation happens in us when our hearts are exposed to the amazing, undeserved, unmerited grace of Jesus. When we feel judged and excluded, we build walls around ourselves to seek protection from the judgment of God and the poor opinion of others. If you really want to see change in your life then it will only happen when we see that having received Jesus, He is no longer judging us for our mess: every sin past, present and future has been paid for. Jesus is using a different grid when He looks at us and that is His finished work of righteousness. Only when we receive that work are we free to let the guard down and receive the healing that we so desperately need. We will live in bondage and condemnation for as long as we believe that Jesus is primarily concerned with punishing us for our wrongdoing.

If you struggle with an area in your life, whether it be habits, patterns of thinking or behaviour, I want to encourage you with this truth - The Lord knows all about it and He does not love you any less because of it. His promises and commitment towards you do not fluctuate based on your performance. His love for you is entirely independent of your actions. At the very moment that you mess up do not turn away from Him in shame, trust that as you turn your face towards Him He is looking on you with only love and compassion; the more that we do that it will help us to receive all that we need to become free.

The big lesson

It is clear here that this woman is a picture for humanity and the plan for grace that sits at the heart of God's purpose for us. The problem is many of us live with a belief that our survival depends on something else other than Jesus, we keep drinking from sources that do not satisfy and so we need to keep returning for more. This manifests itself in many different ways including career, ministry, relationships, education, achievement and a list that goes on and on. The result is that we live exhausted and any sense of wholeness escapes us. It's an obvious point that Jesus is making through this woman; using the imagery of water that we have seen before, He shows that His work goes right to the heart of our condition. This is a question of priority in our lives; the Lord is not saying that any of the things mentioned above, like career, are intrinsically bad, but rather our innermost need will never be met by them alone.

We have heard these words many times so why do we still find it difficult to trust the Lord when He says that by putting Him and His finished work of grace before anything else we will be truly and deeply satisfied? Jesus is reminding us that we were built to live life from the inside out. Our outer worlds are designed to be a reflection of what has been transformed in our innermost place: transformed by grace.

This is what Jesus will go on to say in a chapter that we will examine later:

"If anyone thirsts, let him come to me and drink. Whoever believes in me, as the Scripture has said, 'Out of his heart will flow rivers of living water.'"
John 7:37-38

I am not sure that I have ever met anyone who has really got this in proper order: we are all on the journey of growing in trust with the Lord yet I wish that I could learn more quickly. Much of the difficulty and challenge we face would be easier if we were drawing unearned, unmerited and undeserved favour deep into our hearts every day. We spend a lot of energy trying to improve our circumstances: we spend time and money attempting to derive meaning and purpose from temporal things. The Lord is so gracious that He delivers us daily from some of the poor decisions that we make. This story brings us back to the realisation that there is little satisfaction from anything else unless we are fully satisfied in Him first. I often think how much more enriching and enjoyable work, and everything else, would be if we did not try to have them satisfy what they will never be able to.

Total freedom

In finishing this portrait we see one of the most incredible transformations in the entire Bible. In a religious system that depends on fear and shame to modify behaviour, this stands tall as a sign to the power of grace in our lives. After receiving love and healing there is a deep change in her:

"Come, see a man who told me all that I ever did. Can this be the Christ?"
They went out of the town and were coming to him... "He told me all that I
ever did."
John 4:29-30, 39

Do you want to see change in your life? If you are hungry for transformation then grace is the way.

When I was going to my first kids meeting as a child one of the ways that we would be encouraged to get saved over and over again was by asking us how awful it would be if all our sin, habits and thoughts were displayed on a big cinema screen for the whole world to see. Terrified at the very thought of it I would confess all I could remember and pray that it was enough to turn the wrath of God away from the nine year old that I was.

The woman at the well should be embarrassed and ashamed, but does she sound like a woman that is still locked in her mess? She has just had all her dirty laundry exposed and the result is she feels the greatest sense of freedom and acceptance that she has probably ever felt in her life. She has experienced true transformation, so much so that she runs to the very people that were rejecting her to let them know that she had encountered the purest love and finally found her freedom. We hide ourselves in other distractions because we do not really believe that we are good enough for God to bless and favour. We know our B-roll and dirty laundry, we also know that God is aware of it too. We try to hide and do not turn to the Lord for fear that we will be exposed for all to see.

Can I give you some of the best news that you will ever hear? There is someone who does know you; He knows every single part of you and every thought that goes through your mind: He knows your weakness, He knows your failings, He knows your insecurities, He knows your sin, He knows your inconsistency and He knows your fear: there is absolutely nothing about you that is hidden from Him. In knowing you, He does not reject you nor will He ever humiliate you: the middle of your mess is the perfect place to encounter grace!

This woman discovered someone who knew her completely but whose love was more than enough to transform her from the inside. This was not because of what she had done, but because she was loved by the one who made her. We see that it is not just that His grace is enough to get through: His love is the most powerful gift to tear down the strongest bondage in our lives. That is the life Jesus promised to everyone of us. That is the water that He offers to satisfy beyond anything else. The life that flows from Jesus touches every dry part of our lives to bring it to a place of fruitfulness.

Don't waste another minute looking for answers in things that can't provide what you really need; in Jesus you are not excluded, you are not on the outside because of anything happening in your life. In stepping out of heaven He took the biggest detour ever. He did that to come for you so you could be loved and accepted, transformed by grace and free to live as He always designed.

7

Sustained

"I am the bread of life"
John 6:35

We have had many great experiences with our kids as they have grown up and yet there is one moment that will probably stick with me until I am old and grey. During the first COVID lockdown, we found ourselves trying to figure out homeschooling. Our son was due to take an important set of national exams that form a significant part of the educational journey for 16 year olds. I remember the day when it was announced that these exams had been cancelled and there was no longer any need for the children to sit them. They would be awarded grades based on work already completed, it was simply one of the happiest moments of Ben's life. The smile that filled his face was as wide as is physically possible. He put his pen down in that moment and for weeks after, if you looked into his bedroom, it was as if time had stood still. His school books lay on the desk in the same place, opened at the very page where they had been on that day. We joked about how he had dodged a bullet.

Ben is very bright and academically capable but he would never describe himself as a natural student, school was not his favourite place and to be honest I was pretty much the same. More often than not he would ask me why he would need to know the structure of a leaf, or the content of a Medieval English poem and how useful it would be in real life when he was older. I struggled to answer with any sense of conviction although I do at times find myself quoting random facts to the kids that I learned at school.

There is a point to this that applies to us all: Ben struggled to connect to school as he kept questioning if he was really learning, or just regurgitating facts that had no real relevance to his life.

We often approach the Bible like this: I find it somewhat frustrating after I have finished preaching when somebody lets me know that they have "heard all that before." My question, normally internally and often not vocalised is, "well how is that changing and shaping you?" We can have so much knowledge about the word, but much of it is only information that fills our heads. I am not saying that it's a bad thing, but the Bible uses different words for knowledge that explain the heart of the Lord for us. One word, *gnosis*, means "*a mental ascent to, or an understanding of.*" The other word that Jesus often used was g*inisko*, which means "*knowing through personal experience.*"

When Jesus came it was not that we would simply have an intellectual understanding of who He is, but rather that we would have a living, dynamic relationship experiencing His life in us. Often in pursuit for answers we quickly look for a bite size verse that will give us something to feed on, almost like a motivational quote or an internet meme. Normally this snippet relates to the area we are struggling with, we search for answers and quickly skim through until we find a nugget that we hope will unlock our situation. This is not a criticism, in fact I think we should be pleased when people turn to the word for answers but there is more to it than dipping in when times get tight!

Why is it that we can quote verses and have the "right" answers to the difficult questions but when it comes to actually walking out these promises we feel like there's a gap. There's a disconnect: what we confess to believe and what we see played out can be very different things! When this happens we can feel frustrated, we doubt ourselves, we doubt God and we lose our confidence. That's why we are asking ourselves this question: Who do you say I am? We want to go deeper. We want to get the fuller picture. We want to ignite a passion for the truth. And who is the truth: Jesus Himself.

There is a danger in our Christian walk in thinking that we have heard it all before. It is not only a filling of our minds with knowledge, but a transformation of our hearts that is the result of that knowledge. The Bible is incredibly simple and amazingly complex at the same time. So much so that we will never exhaust all the truth within its' pages. There will always be more of Jesus to be revealed. We are influenced and shaped by what we give our attention to; whatever we magnify becomes bigger in our lives. If you feel like you are not getting answers and are struggling to find the Lord, here's what to do. You have two options: either let the experience drive you away from God, or let it cause you to come closer, to dig deeper:

"If you seek after me you will find me when you seek after me with all your heart."
Jeremiah 29:13

Jesus wants us to see Him in greater ways so that our hearts can be amazed as we stand in awe of who He is. In that place of faith our confidence rises in what He can do; more than that, He wants to go to your core, He wants to satisfy every hunger in your heart.

In these times of uncertainty it is more important than ever that we ground ourselves in the most secure place. When everything around us is being shaken, we need to ensure our foundations are rock solid.

We are looking for answers, looking for solutions, looking for hope. As we go through the book of John, Jesus reveals Himself as the answer to every human need; whether physical, emotional or spiritual. John shows that Jesus came as fulfillment of all the Old Testament prophecies; everything they had learned was pointing to this man. This book was written in such a way that their ears would prick up to the words and phrases that were taken directly from the Torah and prophets; words which they had grown up with, studied and committed to memory: yet even though this was happening before their very own eyes, they couldn't see it. Their hearts were full of pride, they were more interested in their intellectual knowledge of God than actually experiencing Him for themselves.

Your deepest needs

Before Jesus reveals Himself as the "bread of life" we find Him feeding the 5,000. If you have grown up in the church you will have heard this story many times. The problem with that is that rather than engage with the text, our minds revert back to our Sunday school memories. Familiarity can make us dull to the wonder of the details.

It's clearly no coincidence that after Jesus has just physically fed people and satisfied their hunger, He then reveals Himself as being the "bread of life." There are many more significant details throughout these passages and I have been training myself to take a closer look and to think deeper about what they mean. I am no longer satisfied with the bite sized nugget.

The most basic part of this scene that we can overlook is that Jesus is incredibly practical, He understood the needs of the people. He knew their weaknesses and He is exactly the same today. That means that wherever you are reading this, Jesus is the same for you. We need to continually remind ourselves that the Lord knows and understands us: He made us. Your weaknesses don't surprise Him, disappoint Him or limit Him. He also understands our needs, of which the most basic is sustenance.

Have you ever stopped to consider why that is? When we look at the awesomeness of creation it is not that the Lord could not have figured a way for us to survive without this daily need for food, and yet there it is, our most basic need to is to be sustained and survive. We all need food and it's not a monthly or weekly need, it's a daily need. In our house it feels more like an hourly need, we can't switch it off, we can't ignore it and it never goes away.

Sometimes we approach food as a monotonous requirement. Feeding becomes a task that demands time and energy. Yet, think about how food is mentioned in the Bible: it is used as a celebration, a means to connect, relate, fellowship and share together, remember all the details are significant. It was the Passover when the feeding of the 5,000 takes place. People were gathering to celebrate and remember what happened in Egypt. Now the longed for Messiah is walking among them, but how many of them can actually perceive it?

The crowds were on a mountainside in the wilderness. There were no shops close by and we know people were not near their homes or the issue of food would not have been a problem. Hungry people with no access to food and then God shows up in the middle to provide for them. I love what Jesus does here, I think that He's playing a little with His friends. Looking at the crowd He asks them a question: "How are we going to feed all these people?"

I don't think that He was really expecting them to come up with a solution as there was no human way possible to feed every person, I also don't think that He was stuck either. He was setting them up, He was asking them to expand their minds. He was testing them to push them past their natural limitations. He was inviting them to think from a heavenly perspective and see the supply of heaven that was available to them at that moment: He was growing their faith and raising expectation inside them.

As natural men they looked and they were overwhelmed. They saw the issue, the lack and were overwhelmed by impossibility. When Jesus looked at exactly the same situation from a heavenly perspective He saw it differently; He saw the potential and opportunity, He saw the supply.

This is a game changer for your life today: Think about the difficult and impossible situations you are facing. He calls you to step back and look at those situations again. This time He asks you to change the lens that you are looking through. Do you consider your obstacles in the light of the power Jesus has placed within you through His Spirit? Are you drawing from the creative ability that He has placed in you? What is the potential of His grace in you? Look again at your situation through the lens of grace and see how it changes.

Everyday Jesus invites us to go on a journey with Him. One marked by a conviction that He will make a way even when it seems impossible for us. Can you allow yourself to dream with the Lord and imagine new and exciting outcomes? Can you take what it is in your hands and expect it to be multiplied beyond anything you can imagine? Jesus spent His time on earth expanding people's minds to the reality that when He feeds you it is from a supply that is unlimited and most deeply satisfying.

The disciple Andrew here is either brave and full of faith or is completely out of ideas so he thinks he has nothing to lose. He dares to believe and brings the boy with an insignificant packed lunch. Jesus takes the food, gives thanks and it is multiplied. 5,000 men plus women and children are fed and twelve baskets are left over. Everyone is satisfied and there is more than enough. What looked like a huge, insurmountable problem became an opportunity for God to reveal His glory. It's the same for you today, every time you see lack in your life pause and look at it through the lens of grace: What do you see now? Unlimited supply, unlimited resource. It is in these moments that faith grows in us so that we can believe God for His favour to turn around every situation.

And there's more

The next day the crowd were looking for Jesus so they went across the lake to find Him. Jesus had satisfied their physical hunger yet there remained a much deeper hunger in them all. The greater need that God has placed in all of us to be really satisfied, a need that only He can meet. These people were hungry for something more than physical food, they wanted spiritual food: food that meets the deepest longings and desires of their hearts. That is why Jesus reveals Himself in this next discourse as the bread of life.

He is your life source. He is your sustenance. There is nothing that will feed the deepest longing in your heart more than a relationship with Jesus. We know that the need for meaning, purpose and acceptance is universal. Are you making the connection between what you are feeding on spiritually and the impact on your life? We all know when we skip meals and we go without food our bodies feel weak. Eating the wrong food has effects that are obvious within a number of hours. We can't function properly. We do not feel 100 percent. We grow weak and lethargic. We can be more easily distracted and we cannot think straight. We make poor decisions. We get irritable.

It is exactly the same with spiritual food. What are you depending on to bring you hope, wholeness, faith and well being? How many people are weak in their ability to make decisions, how many are distracted, how many are not functioning to their full potential? How many are confused or feeding on things that are causing themselves and those around them harm and pain? You were created to feed on Jesus. You were created with a daily need for Him to nourish you. You were made to draw your true strength through relationship and communion with Him. You were designed to come to Jesus everyday to receive. He is your real supply of what you are looking for.

The law will blind you

Living with a performance mentality means you will struggle to see the fullness of grace. The Rabbi's and the Pharisees reaction to Jesus shows us this clearly:

> *"What must we do to do the works God requires?" Jesus answered, "The work of God is this: to believe in the one He has sent."*
> John 6:28-29

How simple could Jesus make it? The heart of law wants to know what it should do to earn God's approval through performance and works. Jesus showed them how easy it was. All they had to do was to believe in Him yet their response was incredible. It is the next day after this miracle and look at what they ask him:

"What sign then will you give that we may see it and believe you? What will you do? Our ancestors ate the manna in the wilderness; as it is written: 'He gave them bread from heaven to eat.' Jesus said to them, "Very truly I tell you, it is not Moses who has given you the bread from heaven, but it is my Father who gives you the true bread from heaven. For the bread of God is the bread that comes down from heaven and gives life to the world." "Sir," they said, "always give us this bread." Then Jesus declared, "I am the bread of life. Whoever comes to me will never go hungry, and whoever believes in me will never be thirsty. But as I told you, you have seen me and still you do not believe. All those the Father gives me will come to me, and whoever comes to me I will never drive away. For I have come down from heaven not to do my will but to do the will of Him who sent me. And this is the will of him who sent me, that I shall lose none of all those He has given me, but raise them up at the last day. For my Father's will is that everyone who looks to the Son and believes in him shall have eternal life, and I will raise them up at the last day."
John 6:30-40

These men had studied the scriptures, they knew in detail how their God had provided for them in the desert. They read how bread had come from heaven. But they couldn't join the dots to make the picture or perhaps they just did not want to see what was staring them in the face. Jesus was the bread from heaven. He wasn't just there to satisfy their physical hunger, He was there to feed their very souls. "Whoever comes to me will never be hungry." Jesus came to fill that deep hunger in all human hearts. That longing we all know. That need to be connected to our maker. That need to belong. That need to find true meaning and purpose.

Can you see the irony in the Pharisees reaction?

At this the Jews there began to grumble about him because he said, "I am the bread that came down from heaven." They said, "Is this not Jesus, the son of Joseph, whose father and mother we know? How can he now say, 'I came down from heaven'?"
John 6:41-42

It is amazing that they see thousands of hungry people in a desert being supernaturally fed to overflowing and they still complain! I would like to think I would have just sat there with my mouth wide open unable to take in what I had just witnessed. I probably would have questioned whether or not what had just happened was real or had I made it up? It's so amazing. One packed lunch and thousands of people fed. A beautiful picture of how the sacrifice of Jesus would be more than enough for a hungry world. For the many and not the few.

Our condition is one that can never be satisfied outside of the Lord. How often do you hear people moaning and complaining for situations to change and when they do, they moan and complain about the next thing. The difficulty they thought was such a hindrance in their lives can be quickly replaced by the next thing that is not going their way.

Self will never be satisfied. The flesh will never be satisfied. I have gone through days or even seasons when I wanted everything to change. I looked for a sense of peace and happiness. I blamed others, I blamed my poor performance. I thought stuff, friends or positions could satisfy me:

work, money, ministry, relationships, status, reputation, qualifications or whatever else is on your list. None of it lasts and none of it can deliver what we really need.

There is only one source that we can draw from that will meet that deepest need within. But are we ready to humble ourselves? Can we recognise where there is pride in our hearts holding us back from receiving all that the Lord has for us? He won't always turn up in the way we expect and His path won't always look like the one we had imagined.

Grace offends the legalist in us

The Pharisees were offended by Him. They couldn't accept what was staring them in the face, and as He continued He offended them all the more:

"I am the living bread that came down from heaven. Whoever eats this bread will live forever. This bread is my flesh, which I will give for the life of the world."
John 6:51

"Very truly I tell you, unless you eat the flesh of the Son of Man and drink His blood, you have no life in you. Whoever eats my flesh and drinks my blood has eternal life, and I will raise them up at the last day. For my flesh is real food and my blood is real drink. Whoever eats my flesh and drinks my blood remains in me, and I in them. Just as the living Father sent me and I live because of the Father, so the one who feeds on me will live because of me. This is the bread that came down from heaven. Your ancestors ate manna and died, but whoever feeds on this bread will live forever."
John 6:53-58

This was beyond outrageous to those listening. Even today it riles people. How offensive to think that Jesus is the only way to a fulfilled life! Jesus tells us it's His flesh that we need to eat and His blood that we need to drink. This is the picture of His work of grace. The more we receive that truth the more we are satisfied.

The great I Am; The one and only God, who is supreme and above all. He steps out of heaven. He comes and dwells among us. He humbles Himself to death on a cross. His flesh is torn and broken. His blood is poured out and He sacrifices Himself for us. When we accept that He is our bread of life we enter into a life that will last for eternity. We walk into the fullness of life that He has planned since the foundation of the earth.

The Pharisees could not accept this because they were holding onto their good works, their confidence was in their efforts. They felt good about their performance because they could compare themselves with others who were falling further short of the standard than they felt they were achieving. Their system was built on comparison where they always came out on top. They told themselves that even if they were not perfect, at least they were not as bad as others.

Jesus came to destroy this mindset. He took away man's attempts to connect with God and He made it very simple. There was one way - through Him. There was one source of life. He is it!

If you want access to the Father then come to Jesus and feed from Him.

How do we do this?

When Jesus was tempted in the wilderness and tempted to turn stone into bread, what was His response?

Jesus answered, "It is written: 'Man shall not live on bread alone, but on every word that comes from the mouth of God.'"
Matthew 4:4

Every word that Jesus speaks is food to us. John tells us that Jesus is the word. As we feed on Him it is bread to our bodies and souls, we are fed within. I am interested in psychology and science around the mind and the brain. I was listening recently to studies that show the incredible brain activity that happens when people read scripture, literally life can be seen. Think about that for a minute. Your creativity is released, your sense of joy is released, your intellect expands, your ability to reason, your emotions are regulated: this is everything that the world is looking for. So much talk in the world right now is focused on a mental health crisis. Unfortunately society has no real answers to the pain in the human heart. We don't know how to treat people in order to bring true freedom. The word brings life. As we feed on Jesus, our bread of life, we are transformed.

Where are you feeding from today? What are you counting on to nourish you? Jesus says feed on His grace before anything else. He promises He will get to the very heart of what you need and He will satisfy you.

8

Satisfied

"If anyone thirsts, let him come to me and drink."
John 6:37

One of the great joys of having kids is finding yourself in situations that you would rather not be in. When our middle daughter was seven, she came home from school and told us that she could not read the board in the classroom as the writing was blurry. We had not noticed her struggling but in any case we booked an appointment with the optician to get her eyes tested. Penny picked her up from school and they set off to figure out what was happening with her eyesight. On arriving she got settled into the seat and the optician set about displaying different images and letters on the screen, each time checking if Hope could read them clearly. With every image her answer was the same. She simply stared blankly and said that she could not see either the image or the writing. Instead of making the images smaller the optician was making them bigger, yet Hope did not flinch as she calmly answered in the negative to every question she was asked. At this point the images were almost as big as she was. If she couldn't see them then glasses would not have helped, we would have been looking for a guide dog instead!

At this stage the experience of the optician kicked in and she realised what was going on. Going to a drawer she pulled out a pair of glasses and placed them on Hope's nose, it was a miracle. She was healed on the spot and her whole world, apparently, came right back into focus. It was as if she was seeing for the first time. She could read the smallest lettering size from the other side of the room. Left eye, right eye, both eyes. Amazing. What she didn't know was the glasses contained clear lenses and had no effect on what she was seeing. A knowing look was exchanged between Penny and the optician as they explained to Hope that her eyes were okay. Maybe she was just a little tired from all the hard work at school they said to try and help her. The optician asked if any of her friends had got new glasses recently and it transpired that her best friend in school had just got some. At that point it all became clear as to where the sudden onset of near blindness had come from, she just wanted glasses like her friend.

We are sometimes the same; we can look at things and not see them clearly. We need help to get things into focus because when they are not clear, we cannot see the picture as it really is. In this next portrait of Jesus we see something that is not immediately obvious until we get some help to see it more clearly, then the meaning becomes so much richer and will have more impact on our experience of Jesus. Only seeing a blurred image is not something that has only recently afflicted human beings. Jesus was continually revealing Himself as the true Messiah, but they were so wrapped up in a form of religion and their own self righteousness they kept missing what was right in front of their eyes.

We all need a drink

Jesus was never afraid to make a point that He knew would bring deep release and healing to people who needed it. He was not intimidated by position or power and so would often say and do things that would shake what people held dearly. A striking example of this happens in John 7. We have already seen Jesus using the imagery of Himself as water with the woman at the well and in the tabernacle discourse with Nicodemus. Now He goes bigger with the picture and uses one of the most important festivals in the Jewish religious calendar to make a bold declaration that still today resonates with every human heart. There is much incredible richness in this portrait that so I want to take the time to lay it out for you. The details matter. In them we find layer upon layer of revelation about Jesus that is so helpful. When I see the what is woven into these stories, I am encouraged that the intricacies of my life are no problem for God. He knows it all. He never stops working and weaving all of these things together for good.

Booths

To make sure that the picture is clear we first need to understand the context of what was happening when Jesus declared:

"If anyone thirsts, let him come to me and drink. Whoever believes in me, as the Scripture has said, 'Out of his heart will flow rivers of living water.'"
John 7:37-38

The festival of Sukkot occurs after the harvest has been completed and before the beginning of the new agricultural year. There are many parts to it yet there is a sense of welcoming a well deserved rest from labour and genuine rejoicing in what God has done in providing for His people. At Sukkot Jews were called upon to remember God's provision, protection and care since being set free from the bondage and slavery of Egypt. It was also about remembering God's provision during the forty years of wandering in the wilderness.

That is why God told Israel to observe the festival by leaving their permanent dwellings to live in the more fragile, temporary booths or "Sukkot." God instructed Sukkot as a reminder that their dependence upon Him was not something that ended when the Promised Land was reached. Sometimes we think that: we pray for blessing and that is a good thing to do but if we are not careful, once we receive we can forget that it was the Lord who did it in the first place! If we do not guard our hearts then blessing can move us from a place of dependence into a place where we become self reliant, believing that our hard work and effort has brought about the prosperity we are enjoying. Even after a "good harvest," we need to remember the temporary nature of this life and the fact that we ultimately rely on God to provide for us. Sukkot was a reminder that God had chosen to "tabernacle" with them wherever they wandered and that He would be with them no matter where they were.

This was also a forward looking festival. It spoke of the future and this is where it remains relevant to where we are today. Knowing the importance and significance of what is going on Jesus drops an absolute stunning revelation right in the middle of the most momentous part of the whole thing.

Missing the point

Each day of the festival brought many duties for the priests. On the first morning of Sukkot a procession of priests went to the pool of Siloam to bring a golden container of water to the temple. This was sufficient to last throughout the seven days of the feast. Gold in the Bible is the colour of glory, divinity, kingship, eternal deity and righteousness. Water is the picture of the life of God, the Holy Spirit. There is not a single detail wasted in the word. We read:

"On the last day of the feast, the great day."
John 7:37

Why does this matter? The last day was the climax of the festival when the water pouring ceremony took place. Let me describe it to you and try to picture the scene in your imagination: it took place in the temple square which measured about 1/4 mile by 1/4 mile. It would have been absolutely rammed with people. This is a metaphor for the world today, the crowd if you like.

The priests would carry water from the pool of Siloam. As they walked they also sang the words of the Halel Psalms (Psalms 113-118) that contain the words:

"Blessed is He who comes in the name of the Lord"
Psalm 118:26

This verse was known as the welcoming cry of the Messiah. This explains why the crowds sang these very words when Jesus came into Jerusalem in John 12:13, they longed for their Messiah to deliver them. The priests sang these words and at the same time prayed *"Send the rain, send the rain."* This is the future aspect of this ritual as they remember that they needed the blessing of God for their future harvest. There is a deeper meaning here too, this prayer is not just about physical rain but a cry for the Messiah to come. They want deliverance and the rain that they long for is about more than just crops. It is a cry to have their deepest need satisfied and to be delivered from the bondage that grips their lives.

There are three main things happening here: first they are thanking God for delivering them, secondly they are thanking God for the harvest. Harvest here is a metaphor for redemption and a foreshadow of the

75

ultimate redemption that would come through the Messiah. Lastly they are believing for the future because rain literally meant life, without rain there would only be death.

They cannot see what they long for

As the ceremony continued the priest on duty poured out the contents of two silver bowls. Silver is the colour of redemption in the Bible. One bowl held water and the other held wine. This was an act of prayer and an expression of dependence upon God to pour out his blessing of rain upon the earth, the priests did not understand the imagery. Where else do we see this happen in the Word? This was a foreshadow of the crucifixion. On the cross Jesus' side was pierced and blood and water flowed for the redemption of the entire world. I have heard lots of medical explanations for this but I am pretty sure that that was not what John was talking about. It's a picture of Jesus our Redeemer and life literally flowing from Him. The people who originally read this Gospel were looking back at these events having lived through the crucifixion and the resurrection. You can imagine them pulling all the pieces into place and scratching their heads in amazement as all of the details came together. It's like pieces of a jigsaw puzzle being placed bit by bit together to reveal a beautiful picture of Jesus as the Messiah.

On the last day the priests circled the altar seven times (seven being the number of completeness and perfection), they then poured out the water with great pomp and ceremony. This part is called *Hoshana Rabbah*, and the great cry *"HOSHIANA"* was raised, which is translated as "save now." These very same words will be heard once again when the crowd welcome Jesus at his triumphal entry into Jerusalem. *"Hosanna - Blessed is he who comes in the name of the Lord."*

See yourself in the story

How do we apply this today? Let's see the whole picture: people are fervently looking for God, looking for hope, looking for future security, looking for blessing, looking for protection and provision. They do not see that all of that is right there in the person of Jesus, they are too caught up in the ritual of performance. We do the same thing every day. We get so busy putting our faith in what we are doing that we often miss Jesus there in front of us. We busy ourselves in lots of things in the hope that we will be okay tomorrow. Though we are grateful for what the Lord has done up until now, if we are honest we do not always have a confidence for tomorrow, ministry is no exception. We can be surrounded with busyness and a form of religious service and miss Jesus at the same time.

The scene is set for us, religious fervour, ritual and performance. As this is happening Jesus stands up in the middle of the huge crowd that have packed into the temple square. To capture the sense of what He shouts I will paraphrase first:

"I am everything you are looking for... All you are praying for, looking for, all of this work and effort, all of this trying, all of this longing. It is me you need. I will quench your deepest thirst and meet your deepest desire, so come to me"

Let's read it to see the full impact of the words of Jesus in the context of this ceremony:

On the last day of the feast, the great day, Jesus stood up and cried out, "If anyone thirsts, let him come to me and drink. Whoever believes in me, as the Scripture has said, 'Out of his heart will flow rivers of living water.'"

Now this he said about the Spirit, whom those who believed in him were to receive, for as yet the Spirit had not been given, because Jesus was not yet glorified.
John 7:37-39

How much time, energy, money and effort do we spend on searching for true peace? Even ministry cannot take the place of the one that we minster to. The life you need will only ever come from Jesus, in fact it all comes from Him, it does not come from any other source- Not your education, qualifications, bank balance, family, reputation, effort or anything else. You do not have to go year after year replaying the same scenes and crossing your fingers that things get better. As they were looking to their future and saying *"send the rain"* you and I know that we now live in the rain of God's blessing and favour. We see this in the future aspect of the festival of booths.

The word that the Greeks used to translate *"tabernacled with us"* was *skeena.* The Greeks however had borrowed that word in the same way that we do today with other languages. For example the words Faux pas or Mange-tout are words in everyday use that we have borrowed from French. The actual word for *"tabernacled with us"* is "Shakina'd." This talks of when God's glory and very presence would dwell with us. When heaven would meet earth. We now are in the time where we do not need to worry about our future because He is the fulfilment of all that they longed for in this ceremony. His very glory and presence fills us and goes before us. This rain, this water of life is flowing freely to you now because you are loved. It flows from the inside of us. It is His gift of grace, completely unearned and undeserved, flowing in you and around you.

78

Drinking brings fruit

When I taught this in my own church I felt the Lord encouraging me to meditate on Jeremiah 17: it is a beautiful picture of what it is like when we drink this water of life that Jesus promises. What does it look like?

"Blessed is the man who trusts in the Lord, whose trust is the Lord. He is like a tree planted by water, that sends out its roots by the stream and does not fear when heat comes, for its leaves remain green and is not anxious in the year of drought, for it does not cease to bear fruit."
Jeremiah 17:7-8

The picture and promise is clear: No empty religion. No work that is exhausting and unrelenting in its' demands. If we will drink from His grace every day He will satisfy the very deepest needs in our lives. We will prosper no matter what is going around us. This is a promise for you reading this now: the Lord is not limited by your circumstances, your past or your failings. He is not moved by your effort or your performance, He loves you. He promises all you need is already provided because of His love for you. Don't buy into the wisdom of the crowd and the popular opinion of today. Look more clearly at Jesus and His finished work for you and drink from there. Remind yourself that there is only one source of life that will truly satisfy. Whatever the world may promise, nothing will quench our thirst more than His life in us.

9

Switch the light on

"I am the light of the world. Whoever follows me will not walk in darkness, but will have the light of life."
John 8:12

Penny and I got married when we had both just turned 23. I had just graduated from university in Belfast and Penny was continuing her post-graduate study for the first year of marriage. We bought our first house in glorious East Belfast and set about building our life together. Some of the fun, and the challenge, in setting up home together is working out how you each approach normal household stuff. It is a journey of realising how much of your own upbringing shapes your view of the world and what you think is "normal." For example whatever the time of year, I love to open all the windows and let the freezing Irish air blow through the house. It makes me feel alive, Penny however loves to crank up the heating so that it would be possible to grow bananas in the hall! I fear that when our kids are older one of their abiding memories of their mum will be how often she said "close that door, there's a draft!" In recent years we have engaged in thermostat wars. I have found myself tempted to hide the heating control in an effort to keep the temperature somewhere approaching normal. It is like a game of cat and mouse as I turn the dial down and it mysteriously goes up again.

There are lots of other minor irritations that we have laughed our way through in 25 years of marriage. Penny is English and they have a curious habit of putting the milk in the teacup BEFORE pouring the tea. I know of no civilised country on earth where this is even remotely acceptable. Everyone knows that you pour the tea first. There were two cardinal sins that anyone growing up in Northern Ireland would agree are deadly serious, the first was never to leave the immersion heater on. This device was used to heat hot water and legend has it that you would be bankrupt if it was left on for any significant period of time due to the cost of use. One of my favourite Belfast sayings that I heard at a school sports day, was a dad encouraging his daughter by shouting "run like you left the immersion on!" I knew exactly what he meant.

The second is about leaving lights on in the house. I feel like I am becoming more like my own dad with each passing day. I often find that the rest of the family have managed to visit every room in the house and switch on every light in each of those rooms. I am forever walking into rooms and flicking switches off whilst muttering to myself about the electricity bill. I have been known to switch off the lights even when Penny is still in the room. I might leave one on but only after she tells me "Andrew I am actually still in here!" If the kids remember Penny for the reminder of the arctic drafts, they will have the words "Andrew I can't see anything here!" etched into their minds. "We need some light" Penny will remind me. If we don't have light we cannot see.

Light matters

Let's look at John 8 and see how Jesus brings in another symbol to show that the story was all about Him. He has used bread to say that He is the bread of life, He tells us that He is the water of life and now He uses light. In John 8 He announces:

"I am the light of the world. Whoever follows me will not walk in darkness, but will have the light of life."
John 8:12

These words have been used so any times that when we hear them we may not get the magnitude of what Jesus was saying. The word light is *phos* and it means *"the manifestation of God's self existent life, the divine illumination to reveal and impart life."* Imagine what your world without light would be like, many of us have never stopped to think about why light matters.

Light is the very essence of life itself and without it we simply would have nothing. Light is the main source of energy for all living things. I love the first ray of sunrise, the afternoon sun beating down, the glorious spectacle of sunset, the bonfires that we sit around when night falls, the twinkling of stars, the moon that glows. My favourite place in the whole world is the Mourne mountains where at any time of day the light completely changes what you can see in the landscape.

We not only love light but we also need light: We see best in the light and in the darkness we have have limited sight. Exposure to light keeps us healthy and light is used in a number of medical applications to heal and restore brokenness and sickness. Since the beginning of time when God said "let there be light," light has allowed us to live productive lives and has kept the darkness away. Even practically speaking lighting dictates what a space "feels" like. Warm white lights make any space a little more welcoming and comfortable. Colourful lights that twinkle on and off make a space more festive. We can transform any space and create a very specific feeling using light. Light is a big deal. There is something deeply spiritually profound in Jesus describing Himself as the light of the world. Something that will impact you forever.

What's going on here?

At the end of Chapter 7 the Chief Priest and Pharisees had just mocked Nicodemus for suggesting that Jesus' claims might possibly be true. They did not believe anything of what Jesus was saying. Significantly they heaped scorn on Jesus' Galilean origins (John 7:52) Why? They knew from their learning that more than just a prophet was to come from Galilee. As religious scholars they knew what had been written by the prophet Isaiah:

"but later on He shall make it glorious, by the way of the sea, on the other side of Jordan, Galilee of the Gentiles. The people who walk in darkness will see a great light; those who live in a dark land, the light will shine on them"
Isaiah 9:1-2

They held to the belief that when Messiah would come, He would be a great light that would dawn and would dispel the spiritual and physical darkness and bondage that they lived under. The latter portion of this prophecy in Isaiah 9 goes on to describe the Messiah and some of the amazing qualities that would describe Him:

"Wonderful Counsellor, Mighty God, Everlasting Father, Prince of Peace. Of the greatness of his government and peace there will be no end."
Isaiah 9:6-7

Let's have a look at where Jesus was and what was happening. Again when we understand the context of where these portraits take place they become so much more impactful. During the Feast of Tabernacles or Sukkot, there was a great ceremony called the "Illumination of the Temple." This involved the ritual lighting of four golden oil-fed lamps in the Court of Women. These lamps were huge menorahs (another picture of Jesus that they just did not understand) that towered seventy-five feet high over the gathering. They were lit in the temple at night to remind the people of the pillar of fire that had guided Israel in their wilderness journey. All night long the light shone their brilliance. It is said in writings from the time that because of their height and size they illuminated the entire city.

The light from these huge temple lamps was symbolic of two realities: the first was the reality of the "Light of all Lights." This is also known as the 'Shekinah glory' that we read about through scripture. This was the visible presence of God that filled the first temple, built by Solomon (1 Kings. 8:10–11). The second was *Ha'or Gadol*, which means 'the Great Light.' The Jews lived with the belief that *Ha'or Gadol* would come and bring light to those who were spiritually dead and dwelling in darkness as written in Isaiah 9:2. This festival was a reminder that God had promised to send a light; the Light, to a broken and dark world. They held to the promise that God would send the Messiah to renew Israel's glory, release them from bondage and restore their joy.

Imagine with me that you are in ancient Jerusalem during the Feast of Tabernacles: can you see in your mind what it would be like to see these massive menorahs giving a tremendous amount of light over the temple and city? It must have been a hugely impressive sight. Now imagine the impact of those words said by Jesus in the temple courtyard when He announced, *"I am the Light of the world."* He was saying He is the Light, the source of illumination to bring the lost out of darkness. Jesus declared Himself to be the Light of the world. He is *Ha'or Gadol,* the one that they were longing for. The menorah, as big and impressive as they appeared, were only a man made attempt to represent the glory of God that now stands in the midst of them. He announces that He is their Redeemer. He will remove the darkness and restore them to fullness. People would have been stunned by this, in fact outrage does not come close to describing how they would have felt towards Him. However this was more than just words from Jesus, He shows the people what happens when this Light touches darkness.

Jesus shows us the power of light

Shortly afterwards Jesus is teaching in the temple court treasury. A woman, who was in a terrible situation of her own making, is brought to him and thrown at His feet. Her fate appeared sealed and it was almost certainly death. She was hopeless. Her life was surrounded in darkness at this moment. What will happen when this darkness collides with Jesus, the light? He demonstrates what the light and life of God looks like when we are in need. Although not at first willingly, the woman "will come to the light" while her accusers will shrink away into the shadows.

We are the woman

We often turn from Jesus when we mess up and yet He is the very one that we should be turning to. If we think that God is the source of our condemnation then the ensuing shame will cause us to turn away from Him. This woman had been caught in the act of adultery. Nobody is in any doubt that she is guilty, she has been caught in the very act of sin and it's not just a small one either. Adultery does not seem like a huge deal today, it has almost been normalised. It is serious enough to be included in the 10 commandments and in the times of Jesus was a capital offence punishable by death. Even in engagement would the rules regarding adultery apply to the couple. This woman was facing certain death. The crowds were angry and they had found a victim that would satisfy their bloodlust.

The entire situation was desperate for the woman. She had been dragged to this place half-naked, manhandled and thrown to the ground by a crowd of angry men. Her guilt is compounded with fear, shame and humiliation. In the truest sense of the word, she was condemned. In the eyes of the law she had done wrong and now she had to face the consequences of her actions and be punished. We all know that we have lived far from perfect lives, though not many of us have had to live with our failure so publicly on display and with such dire consequences as a result. We each understand guilt, shame and condemnation however.

The ugliness of legalism

On the other side you have the horrible effects of law. In the crowd we see anger, jealousy, gross hypocrisy, deception, pride, hate, self righteousness, cruelty, selfishness and a total lack of mercy. In fact it's like five minutes of reading Twitter! We see the true ugliness of self righteousness and judgement yet what plays out is one of the most beautiful pictures of grace in the whole Bible.

We see the light of grace shining on brokenness. Living in law does not create the power to change. It simply creates a strengthening of sin and the opportunity for pride and hypocrisy to run rampant, with death as the result. How do you spot a legalist? They are more concerned with rule keeping and finger pointing than they are with relationship and people. Do not get me wrong, I believe that sin is serious and can only be dealt with through the grace of Jesus, but grace is never an excuse to sin. People who use the grace of God as cover for willful sinful behaviour have not truly had a revelation of grace. The Word tells us that grace frees us from the power of sin and does not deliver us into sin.

The point is that for all their rule keeping and knowledge of God's law they did not care one bit about the woman. That is a hallmark of a legalistic heart. The rules are promoted over relationship and behaviour is promoted over identity. People become less important than being right and love is hard to find. Motives are not about God's love for an individual but rather people become objects to be used and abused in order for a point to be made. This woman was secondary to the issue at hand, her sin. She was not seen as a daughter but her identity was reduced to the sum of her sin.

The contrast of grace

"By this all people will know that you are my disciples, if you have love for one another"
John 13:35

This is both encouraging and challenging. What should you and I be known for? Simply it is love. Our selfless love commitment to the Lord which then flows to one another is what should define the people of God. Who we allow a place of influence in our lives has a marked impact on how well we live like this. Think about the people who speak into your life, what marks those people out? Is it their razor sharp insight into other people's faults? Their critical analysis of others' shortcomings? Or is it because after you have spent time with them you come away encouraged about the love, grace and mercy of God and an excitement for Jesus and His church?

Legalistic, critical hearts don't really care about people, restoration, redemption, or healing. The point is that law is serious. Legalism left to run riot in your heart will only ever result in death, in this case the death of this woman.

The potential traps

This whole episode was a set-up aimed at trapping Jesus. A look at the scene tells us what is really going on, the legalists ignored huge swathes of the law so that they could concentrate on the parts that supported their cause. That is often how it works. The legalist's faults and failures are overlooked in the desperate desire to be right and prove someone else wrong. There are three areas that they chose to ignore. First of all where was the man? Deuteronomy 22:22 says that both the man and the woman caught in adultery should die, yet he is nowhere to be found.

Secondly, how did they catch her? It was clear that she was caught in the act so were they looking through a window at a woman having sex? The word is clear that "you shall not covet your neighbour's wife." These men were guilty under the very same law that they had weaponised. It has been suggested that perhaps the woman was also set up although it is not clear that is the case. Finally, if Mosaic law commanded her to be stoned, why did they not just do that? They couldn't take matters in to their own hands because Roman law prohibited it. If Jesus agreed that she should die, He would have been guilty of breaking Roman law. The legalists set multiple traps for Jesus in the hope that He would incriminate Himself, they are not interested in the well being of the woman at all. She is simply a pawn in their game.

A masterclass in grace

At this point we can feel the tension in this story, the crowd would have become quiet as all eyes fell on Jesus. The question they are asking is "What will He do?" What is He going to say? Will He take the bait and condemn the woman? Will He side with them in their self righteous crusade? As we watch this masterclass of grace unfold we see that Jesus employs a really interesting strategy for negative, legalistic people - He ignores them completely. How much time and attention do you give to people - either if they accuse you or if they are accusing others in your presence? We could do well to learn from Jesus here. As He kneels we see Him writing in the ground. There have been many guesses as to what He wrote but we do not know. The image though of Jesus mirroring the finger of God writing the law on tablets of stone is one which would not have been lost on the crowd.

Jesus tells the crowd if they want to live by the law then they will have to go the whole way, no half measures allowed. "Cast the first stone" is a challenge that nobody was prepared to take. Jesus knew the law better than they did. If you were the person to bring the accusation then you had to be the first person to impose the penalty. So who had actually seen her? No one responds to the challenge from Jesus.

If you brought a false accusation the accused could demand the same penalty be applied to you: we could all do well to listen here because when we point the finger, slander, gossip, backstab and judge then the same measure applies back to us. There is a cost when we lower ourselves to that behaviour. The crowd remains still. They know they are not dealing with somebody who is unaware of the law and its demands. Moments pass and yet still nobody moves - were they guilty? At least in their hearts they had coveted another woman and so from the oldest to the youngest they turn and leave, heads bowed in silence.

It is important to note here that Jesus did not condemn the crowd and neither did He threaten them. He knows the power of the law to condemn. Whenever we judge ourselves against the perfect demands of the law there is no way that we can come away without guilt. We all know where we have fallen short and missed the mark.

When grace collides with the legalism in your life and in others, it shows us that we are all in the same boat. Grace is a great leveller. It shows us a much better way than the cycle of defeat, failure and self righteousness that self-sufficient law keeping brings. Without having to point out individuals in the crowd, encountering Jesus showed them what was in their hearts. They did not fight, argue or try to defend themselves. They knew what they knew. Many of them would have gone away that day with a genuine revelation of their own shortcomings. This is what happens when we encounter grace. It makes all the reckoning of our own righteousness rendered obsolete in the light of His love.

The gift of no condemnation first

She had committed a capital offence, she was guilty there was no doubt about that. We see what it looks like when Jesus, the Light of the world, encounters the darkness in our lives. For years I struggled with what Jesus did here: I was taught that, as long as I behaved correctly, then I belonged. We too often want the outward signs of right living before full acceptance or approval is given. Grace upsets the order and turns our small minded legalistic thinking on its head. What does Jesus do that we need to receive for ourselves? I always imagined that the Lord would start her recovery by pointing out her faults and what she had to do to clean herself up. The crowd won't condemn her because they know they stand condemned themselves. But Jesus, What will He say? The answer is staggering: "Neither do I condemn you." In your very worst moments, whenever the sin of your life comes crashing down around you, when the private becomes public on display for the world to see, Jesus does not condemn.

Why is that? the prophet Isaiah 700 years before Jesus was born had written about the Messiah who would deliver the people:

"But he was pierced for our transgressions; He was crushed for our iniquities, upon Him was the chastisement that brought us peace,and with his wounds we are healed."
Isaiah 53:5

There is nothing here that says that sin is not serious and that grace is an excuse for sin. Jesus wants you and I to be free from sin and all of its' consequences. The real question is how do we get to the point of freedom? Jesus offers this woman the most freeing gift of all - the gift of no condemnation. Isaiah tells us that He would take on Himself the weight of all our sin and carry it from us. I have often said that if you want to know what is really in your heart then remove the threat of punishment. Once we no longer feel that we will be punished for our mess then we feel safe enough to open up to the light of God's love that will forgive us, heal us and restore us. When the threat of punishment remains, we try to keep sin hidden and keep ourselves locked in darkness and defeat. Jesus knows that if this woman can receive grace then she will learn to walk free from the sin that has blighted her life.

We need to know that Jesus stands full against sin in our lives. He hates what it does to the ones He loves. Having received Him He will never condemn us again for our sin but He does not condone it either. He shows us that His love and grace are the only ways to break free from the power of sin. After she has received this gift of no condemnation He is absolutely clear - 'go and sin no more.' He assures her that there is no punishment and she has nothing to fear. This is what enables her to leave sin behind, the order is critical. If we understand that we are free from punishment and then we will live free. Punishment is different from consequences, poor decision making can create difficulties for us but that does not mean that He is punishing us. In fact His grace leads us out of the situations that our sin put us in in the first place. Religion reinforces the darkness instead of bringing light. Many of us never find freedom because we are afraid to come to the light. We think that the light will expose us, illuminating our mess. However the light heals us. Jesus tells us that we will not stop sinning because we are afraid of being stoned but because we have encountered grace. After we receive grace repentance and true transformation happen.

This discovery of light in our lives is transformational. The apostle Paul in Romans 8 describes it so clearly. As you read this encourage yourself that when the word says that 'nothing will separate you from the love of God,' it means just that - absolutely nothing. That includes your sin. Once you have received Jesus as your own Saviour then the only light that Jesus shines into your life is to illuminate what you have become as a new creation. His light is about showing you that you are now righteous. When we receive that truth we will no longer want to live in any kind of sin:

"So, what do you think? With God on our side like this, how can we lose? If God didn't hesitate to put everything on the line for us, embracing our condition and exposing himself to the worst by sending His own Son, is there anything else He wouldn't gladly and freely do for us? And who would dare tangle with God by messing with one of God's chosen? Who would dare

even to point a finger? The One who died for us—who was raised to life for us!—is in the presence of God at this very moment sticking up for us. Do you think anyone is going to be able to drive a wedge between us and Christ's love for us? There is no way! Not trouble, not hard times, not hatred, not hunger, not homelessness, not bullying threats, not backstabbing, not even the worst sins listed in Scripture: They kill us in cold blood because they hate you. We're sitting ducks; they pick us off one by one. None of this fazes us because Jesus loves us. I'm absolutely convinced that nothing—nothing living or dead, angelic or demonic, today or tomorrow, high or low, thinkable or unthinkable—absolutely nothing can get between us and God's love because of the way that Jesus our Master has embraced us."

Romans 8:31-39

That is what it is like to live in the light!

10

I AM

"I AM who I AM... This is my name forever"
Exodus 3:14-15

There is nothing like a bit of pressure to change a situation. If you have never played golf you may struggle to understand just how easy it is to make a complete fool of yourself when playing. It's part and parcel of this game that I love. Many years ago when I was just starting out I went for a round at a local club with three other friends. I had a new trolley and a shiny new set of clubs. To top it off I was dressed like I had just fallen from the pages of a golfing catalogue. After a few warm up swings at the driving range I was ready to go, it was a Friday evening in Summer which meant that the course was really busy. Groups of golfers stood outside the pro shop waiting for their turn at the first tee. They were talking and laughing, excited about the prospect of playing a round after a hard week at work. It was at this point I realised this might not be as easy as I had first thought. I had never experienced first tee nerves before and as our turn approached I started to sweat and feel very nervous. My head was spinning. I was about to perform in front of all these experienced golfers. "How hard could it be?" I thought. I totally looked the part. I had all the right gear and there was nothing to suggest that I was out of my depth.

My three friends all took their shots and found the middle of the fairway, it was my turn and I was feeling serious pressure. I put the ball on the tee and my heart was beating so fast that I thought I was going to pass out. I pulled the club back and took a whack at the ball. What happened next will never leave me. It was a shot in a million. To this day I think if I tried to do it again I would not be able to pull it off. As the club connected with the ball it went almost perfectly at 90 degrees to the right from where I was standing and hit a huge tree that covered the tee box. I think it broke some law of physics in terms of how it travelled. From that point everything happened in slow motion. The ball continued at warp factor ten and went behind me, where it bounced off the window of the pro shop. Twenty five golfers hit the ground as the ball pinged off the buildings like it was in a pin ball machine. It was really loud for some reason, in horror I watched as it all unfolded in slow motion before me.

When it came to a stop it was like a scene from a disaster movie. No one made a sound. Slowly, one by one, the golfers lifted their heads to see if it was safe for them to get up. I was stuck to the spot and didn't know what to do. No one made a sound. They were in stunned disbelief at what had just happened. There was no way that I was going to risk trying another shot so I went to my trolley, looked at the collection of faces staring at me and said out loud the first thing that came to my mind - "Thank you." I nodded in different directions as they continued to look at me in disbelief. Still not a word was muttered. I didn't even look at my friends as I set off down the fairway quietly praying for the rapture to take me. Only at the green did we laugh so hard at the fact that I nearly took out a group of golfers with just one ball. That is the joy of playing golf.

Functional Gods - Who sits at the centre of your life?

Pressure can uncover something very profound about us. We all have a view about who we are. I have heard it said though that if you truly want to know yourself, then that is most likely revealed when you are under pressure. This is especially true when it comes to faith. Pressure reveals more than anything else about what we really believe to be the most important thing in our lives. Many of us live in the tension of two positions. What we really want to believe about Jesus, and what we actually believe. The difference is that what we actually believe is predominantly what we will see manifest when we are under pressure. We have learned the right words to say but what we turn towards in dependency, particularly in moments of pressure, shows us our "functional God." This is nothing new to human beings. Many great thinkers and writers have expressed this dilemma.

Martin Luther, the great church reformer said: *"Whatever your heart clings to and confides in, that is really your god, your functional saviour."*

Tim Keller, author of The Reason for God, said something very similar: *"If anything becomes more fundamental than God to your happiness, meaning in life, and identity, then it is an idol."*

Ken Sande said, *"Most of us think of an idol as a statue of wood, stone, or metal worshiped by pagan people....In biblical terms it is something other than God that we set our heart on, that motivates us, that masters and rules us, or that we trust, fear or serve.....An idol can also be referred to as a 'false god' or a 'functional god.'"*

To make it really simple, a functional god is anything we reach for in our lives that is more central, important or fundamental to our identity, other than Jesus and what He says about us. They are what we are *actually* relying on. There are so many things to choose from when it comes to functional gods - money, power, achievement, education, ministry and physical beauty among countless other things. There's a very long list of what we turn to for safety, protection and purpose.

Living in this tension is very common. I believe that most of us do want to live with Jesus at the centre; to experience Him shaping, forming, leading, guiding and developing us is a noble desire. The global COVID pandemic is one example of how pressure forced us to look at what was really important. What was it that gave way in your life during that time? Sadly many people stopped attending church as they simply found that it was not as important as they thought it was. Money is another example, we worry about provision so we cut back, or stop altogether, in our giving. Generosity is squeezed in uncertain times, what does that show us? Whatever we say we believe, our job or employer is serving as a functional god - our source of supply. That is what we are putting our faith in. The problem with functional gods is that no matter what they are they will never deliver what they promise. Jobs can change. Organisations can reshape and resize, there is always someone smarter. Achievement in and of itself never satisfies but leaves a craving for more. The bold claims of functional gods to satisfy the needs of the human heart are nothing more than fake news.

This is not in any way about making you feel condemned. It is instead understanding that as a child of God you have much better promises for your life than anything the world can offer. 1st Peter 1:13 says:

"set your hope fully on the grace that will be brought to you at the revelation of Jesus Christ."

Our best life is only found in grace that comes as our understanding of Jesus grows. That is who we are to set ourselves fully on. In the middle of a volatile, uncertain, complex and ambiguous world, Jesus is speaking to us. For those who do not know Him what He says sounds outrageous. For those of us who profess Him as Lord, it challenges where our faith really lies. Either way you will see from this next revelation of Jesus that there is a deeper grace for you; a life of favour that He is drawing you towards as you experience more of His love. These are times to let God lead you to a deeper revelation of His love for you. It is all encompassing and is the answer for every anxiety and burden.

I AM? - Help me with that

The background will help us understand what Jesus was talking about. Let's go all the way back to the book of Exodus. In Chapter 3, God appeared to Moses in the form of a burning bush and told him that He was going to send Him to free the Israelites from slavery. Moses was initially pretty sceptical and not at all excited by the thought of this task. Why? He worried that the people would not believe that God had sent him. He needed reassurance, so he enquired of God:

> "*if they ask me, 'What is his name?' what shall I say to them?*"
> Exodus 3:13

Up until this point, the Israelites called their God Elohim or El. This was not a personal name. It was a title. They also used "El Shaddai" which is translated as "God Almighty." Moses was familiar with the names of dozens of Egyptian gods like Ra and Anubis as he had been raised from a child in the Egyptian court. He asked God for His name as Pharaoh would want to know on whose name and authority he was being petitioned to set the people free.

After killing an Egyptian he ran away to Midian. Here Moses would have also learned the names of the Canaanite gods such as Baal and Asherah. What is common between the Egyptian and Canaanite gods is that they were individually associated with a particular area of life. Ra was the Egyptian sun god, Baal was the god of war. Asherah was the god of fertility. But what about God? What about Elohim? What does He reply? When Moses asked God for His name, the response was probably not what he was expecting:

> "*I AM WHO I AM... This is my name forever*"
> Exodus 3:14-15

This response set God apart from all the other gods that the people knew. He was declaring that He is not limited to a first name or a particular area of life. He was not made by human hands nor given a name by human beings. This incredible declaration "I AM" comes from the Hebrew verb "*to be or to exist.*" In one statement He declared that He is self existent, eternal, self sufficient and unchanging.

This statement also declared that He is present with us (His people) and not distant from us. His people were in slavery and He was not ignorant of their plight. He wanted to deliver them, to bless them and establish them forever as an example to the nations that He is the one true God (Exodus 3:7–15). When God revealed His name it showed that He is a God who desires an intimate relationship with those He created. First names were often only shared in covenant relationship.

It is from this statement "I AM WHO I AM" that the Holy name of God Yahweh is formed. This name was considered so holy that it could not be spoken aloud or even written in full. Jewish scribes would only ever write the name once with a quill and then they would break it afterwards, so holy was it to them.

Jesus causes a stir (again)

This is the context in John 8:58 where Jesus causes an absolute scandal among the Jews. He said "*Truly, truly, I say to you, before Abraham was, I am.*" In this one sentence Jesus identified Himself as God. This was so incendiary that they wanted to kill Him for blasphemy. The Jewish leaders heard the message loud and clear. This Rabbi is saying that He is God. However in no way was Jesus guilty of their accusation of blasphemy. Colossians 1:17 tells us that Jesus was not created but is self existent, He is eternal, He is self sufficient and Hebrews 13:8 tells us that He is unchanging - "*Jesus Christ is the same yesterday, today and forever.*"

What does this mean for us for us today?

In a world full of "gods," Jesus declares that HE is the one true God over all. He is the source. He is the beginning and the end. They are fine words but there is a very practical outworking of that. The revelation will change you profoundly.

I AM x7

In the Gospel of John, Jesus makes seven statements beginning with the words "I am." Each time our understanding of who Jesus is and His ministry to us grows deeper. If we could allow these truths to change our hearts and thinking we wouldn't be tempted to look to other functional gods that are nothing but a poor imitation. I love that there is nothing in the word that is there by accident. Seven in the Bible is the number of completeness and perfection on both a spiritual and physical level.

It is tied directly to God's creation of all things. In the created world there is one above it all who has your every need already provided for. We should not depend on idols that will only disappoint, but on the one who was from before the beginning and who is holding your life and future now.

Whenever Jesus made an "I am" statement He claimed an attribute of God. He was clearly identifying Himself as God. This so enraged the religious leaders. Each statement is a picture of how the Lord is looking after a different part of your life. When all seven are put together we see a picture of divine covering that is perfect and complete.

Where do we start? It is hard to believe for blessing in our lives if we struggle with the basics. The need for physical provision is completely supplied by the Lord. Jesus declared:

"I am the bread of life"
John 6:35

He establishes a pattern that helps us to see words proven through action. This is the pattern, He makes a statement about who He is and He backs it up with something He does. When Jesus says He is the bread of life He had just fed the 5,000 in the wilderness. At the same time, He contrasts what He can do in the covenant of grace with what Moses had done for the people of Israel when under the law:

"Our ancestors ate the manna in the wilderness, yet they died. But here is the bread that comes down from heaven, which anyone may eat and not die"
John 6:49–50

Jesus is your "bread of life." Just as bread sustains us physically, He promises to sustain us physically and spiritually. There is nothing that will satisfy our innate spiritual hunger more than a relationship with your maker. People get involved in all sorts of craziness to try and meet that need. You don't need to look elsewhere for spiritual nourishment. He is your life! All you need to do is believe in Him and to receive.

This second of Jesus' "I am" statements comes right before He heals a man born blind. He says:

"I am the light of the world"
John 8:12

Jesus not only says He is the light; He proves it. We see here an echo of God Himself back in the original creation story in Genesis 1:3, *"And God said, 'Let there be light,' and there was light."* You don't have to live in darkness, hopelessness and bondage to sin with all of its evil consequences. He will bring His light into your life, transforming you from the inside out.

Our world is increasingly insecure. Our hope goes beyond just what we see around us. Jesus declared:

"I am the door"
John 10:7

He is the way to great hope and eternal security. No one and nothing else will provide you with that deep sense of safety other than Jesus. His words here are are illustrated in the imagery of sheep going into a sheepfold. There is only one way in and that is through Him. Other functional Gods may promise a secure future but none of them can deliver it. This is why I love the message of grace, we often think that we are the door to security through our own effort and hard work. Jesus says differently.

We all are desperate for protection, safety and supply in our lives. The global COVID pandemic showed us what happens when people feel that these are in doubt. I would say that there are still people working their way through the surplus of toilet roll that was bought in bulk during lockdown. In fact I imagine that they are probably still eating bowls of pasta for dinner each night given the huge quantities that were stockpiled. I am not mocking but we see how people can respond when they feel threatened. What does Jesus say?

"I am the good shepherd"
John 10:11

He shows His deep love and care for you. He is the One who willingly protects His flock even to the point of His own death. When Jesus called Himself the good shepherd, there was no mistaking that He was taking one of God's most well known titles from the Old Testament:

"The Lord is my shepherd"
Psalm 23:1

As I get older I find myself thinking about the fact that at some point I am going to not be around anymore. Perhaps it is a stage of life thing and I am certainly not believing that this will be anytime soon, but it does cross my mind. I was watching a TV programme with Penny one evening when a feeling of dread suddenly came over me. It was probably because there was lots of people meeting their end in the show we were watching. However the Lord ministered to me in that moment that He is the greatest power. There is nothing more powerful that I will ever know. Jesus said:

"I am the resurrection and the life"
John 11:25

After this He raised Lazarus from the dead. Jesus' teaching was not just empty words. It's one thing to make a claim but something else entirely to back it up with action - especially when it involves bringing the dead back to life. We read that He holds:

"the keys of death and the grave"
Revelation 1:18

When He raised Lazarus from the dead He showed how He can fulfill Yahweh's promise to ancient Israel:

"God's dead shall live; their bodies shall rise"
Isaiah 26:19

Outside of Jesus, there is neither resurrection nor eternal life. In that moment I felt such a sense of peace fill me as I realised that my hope is secure and that however great this life may be it is only a glimpse compared to where I am going.

Hope and certainty seem like they are in short supply today. In the post truth world we inhabit, the very notion that we can be sure about anything is deemed laughable. Truth has become so malleable as to be rendered meaningless. The idea that there is truth beyond a personal subjective view is increasingly unpopular.

Is there a solid foundation to build your life on? Is there an external point of reference, a north star if you like, for you and I to measure against so we know not just where we are but where we need to be? Jesus said:

"I am the way, the truth and the life"
John 14:6

This powerful "I am" is packed with meaning and today is considered very controversial. How can anyone claim to be the only truth? Jesus clearly says that He is the only way to God. There is no other route. He is proclaiming that He is the truth therefore confirming His identity as the Word of God (John 1:1). The word that Jesus uses for truth is *alethia*, the same word in John 8:32 when He says:

"you will know (experience) the truth (alethia) and the truth (alethia) will set you free"

The message is clear, Jesus is our external reference point. He is our true north. There is much more than our personal experience, as important as that is. Our view and opinions matter but they are not the final truth. If we want an objective view of what is true or not then we will only ever find that in Him, living from that place brings us freedom.

Lastly Jesus says that He sustains you in all things with the declaration:

"I am the true vine"
John 15:1

I am going to expand this in a later chapter but the final metaphorical "I am" statement emphasises the life sustaining power of Jesus. We are the branches, and He is the vine. That is a binary statement with profound implications for how we live. A branch cannot bear fruit unless it is joined to the vine, meaning that the only way that we can bear fruit is to stay connected to Him, everything we need comes from one source.

Pressure will always be a part of life. Not all pressure is negative. On a positive note it can be a motivator for action and compel us to adapt, change and do something that we might not want to do otherwise. Often it shows us what is really going on inside of us. Pressure shows us what is truly important to us regardless of the image we try to portray to others. Pressure will either bring us to grace or drive us from it. The good news is that we have an answer for every area of our lives, both now and forever. It would be good to reflect on that for yourself.

What do you turn to when the pressure comes?

How do you respond?

Do you turn to Jesus, or from Him to other things?

Jesus says that He is self existent, eternal, self sufficient, self directed and unchanging. He is God, He is truth and there is none other like Him. Whatever your need right now you can relax knowing that Jesus is all you need. Every area of your life has a promise of grace written over it, and those promises never fail. They reveal to us the only true God and His Son Jesus - the great I AM.

11

A different kind of shepherd

"He will tend His flock like a shepherd; He will gather the lambs in His arms."
Isaiah 40:11

One of the funny things I remember about primary school were the annual visits by health professionals. They carried out annual checks to make sure the children were in good physical health. For the younger kids, parents were usually present to help, incase any child became unsettled in the examination. I remember getting one of my first hearing tests, and causing total panic in the young nurse, my mum who was there in support. It should have been a simple enough, the nurse placed a set of headphones over my ears and gave me a ruler in my hand. She then gave me simple instructions - *"Andrew, when you hear a beep like this.... (a beep then sounded in my headphones).... I want you to hit the desk with the ruler."* So simple. She went back to her control station and I didn't take my eyes off her. In anticipation I waited for the first beep.

The first sound was much lower in volume than the test beep, so I didn't hit the desk. She had told me that I should only do that when I heard a beep that was the same as the first one. I took that literally. This one was lower in volume so I did not move. She made a note in her book, turned the big dial, and another beep filled the air. Again, I didn't move as it was still not the same as the first one. She made another note and turned the dial a few notches. I stared at her without batting an eyelid. This repeated for another couple of cycles and by this stage it was really loud in my ears. But I had been told – "only bang the desk when you hear the same beep as the first one." The ruler in my hand never moved. Finally, she cranked the dial all the way up to eleven. My eyes were watering and I'm nearly sure my ears bled, as the loudest noise I had ever heard pierced my eardrums! But still my hand didn't move.

In a panic the nurse rushed over to me, lifted the earphones off my head, and asked my mum how she hadn't noticed that her son was deaf. My mum was somewhat surprised as this was news to her. Taking my head in her hands, the young nurse looked at me and mouthed very slowly "Can you hear this Andrew?" I immediately replied "Yes." The nurse jumped back and my mum looked relieved. They asked me why I had not banged the desk when I heard a beep. "*They were louder or softer than the first one*" I replied, "*So I was waiting for the same sound to happen again.*" It was not what I was expecting so I did not respond. The joy on my mum's face was priceless as she realised that I was perfectly healthy. As for the nurse I'm not so sure she felt the same way.

The law is no laughing matter

Life can be like that. We can be confronted with the obvious and still miss it. How did the religious leaders totally miss who Jesus was, even though He was right in front of them? The root of the problem was their hardness of heart. They were so stubborn that a blindness covered their spiritual eyes to that which should have been obvious. They were going about their rituals, engaged in the duties and ceremonies that God had given to point them to this very moment when the Messiah they longed for would come. Yet when He steps into their world they could not recognise Him.

He was not what they imagined. They were looking for physical freedom from the occupying government but He did not meet their expectations. Jesus came to expose the darkness in the human heart and deliver us from the bondage of sin. There's an incredible contrast here, as the Pharisees refuse to accept what is staring them in the face and continue to operate in the shadows. These incidents build a vivid portrait of the beauty and majesty of the kingdom of light, as compared to the cruelty and harshness of a religious system that operates in the darkness. These bad shepherds who exploited and intimidated the people are the very antithesis of everything that God intended for His children. They managed a religious system that put an unbearable burden on the people. It demanded more than anyone would be capable of doing. To make things worse, they were a bunch of hypocrites who could never live up to the standards they professed. It is against this backdrop that Jesus reveals Himself as the Good Shepherd.

A man born blind

There is something so powerful in this next portrait of Jesus. Let's get into this story where the disciples and Jesus encounter a man blind from birth. It's interesting how this narrative starts, as this blind man becomes an object of discussion among the disciples. They ask Jesus:

"Rabbi, who sinned, this man or his parents, that he was born blind?"
John 9:2

We see it's a ridiculous question. If the man was born blind, then how could he have sinned before he was born? It shows the mindset of religion. The disciples operated in this highly religious culture that says a transgression against the law results in a price that must be paid. The encounter exposes a preoccupation with apportioning blame. The first concern was not to see this man set free, he was the subject of a theological debate. The law looks for the cause, rather than the solution! There is no compassion in the law, it is unbending in what it demands. It is not designed to set someone free, but to show each and everyone equally that they are guilty. Today when people operate with a legalistic mindset they are mostly concerned with blame, and the punishment that follows. We are pre-wired to believe that if a mistake has been made, then someone needs to 'pay for it.'

Contrast this with Jesus' reaction: He sees the person first, and they are not defined by their mistakes, they are more than that. He sees the problem, but provides the solution. He is not limited by the mess. His heart is to bring freedom, to redeem and to heal. He looks at the very same situation and sees an opportunity to show love and restoration.

He responded to their question saying:

> *"Neither this man nor his parents sinned,.... but this happened so that the works of God might be displayed in him."*
> *John 9:3*

What Jesus does next is certainly a bit out there. He spits on the ground, makes mud, and places it on the man's eyes. He then tells him to go and wash in the pool of Siloam. The man does as Jesus says and miraculously he is able to see.

Some things in the Bible definitely make us stop and ask why? This is one. Why did Jesus do the whole mud and spit thing? He could have simply commanded healing, that strikes me as being a bit easier. Some say it was to show that Jesus was not constrained by the Sabbath, as it was forbidden to make clay on that day. Others argue that this was meant to parallel God's original creation of man:

"The LORD God formed the man from the dust of the ground"
Genesis 2:7

In other words, Jesus was showing His power as the Creator by imitating the original creation of man: He used the "dust of the ground" to give new sight to the man born blind.

Either way, you would think the news of this miraculous healing would warm the hearts of all who heard it. When the news reaches the religious leaders, they are anything but delighted! They instead interrogate the man and his family. They are not rejoicing that a miracle has taken place. This man whose life had been one of darkness, has now been completely transformed. He is literally walking in the light, yet the religious leaders are angered by his claims and they want him silenced. That shows how warped a religious mindset can be.

They start with the parents and threaten them with expulsion from the temple. Their influence is so powerful that even his own mother and father fear the thought of being rejected by the religious leaders. They take no responsibility, saying the man is old enough to speak for himself. How crazy this is, if your son had been healed of blindness would you not be telling everyone the good news? I saw how delighted my mum was when she discovered that I wasn't deaf. Yet so great was the intimidation from religion, they feared for themselves. To be

111

excluded by the authorities was a terrible thing. You would be cut off from social relationships and connection, but greater than that was being made to feel that God Himself did not accept you. These leaders acted like the gatekeepers who decided who could be called children of God.

It's easy for us to read this story and feel indignant towards the parents. Who in their right mind would allow this manipulation and control? Yet many Christians today are living in bondage, and allow manipulation and intimidation to dominate their lives. The fear of rejection is such a powerful force. We are all born with the need to feel safe and to feel that we belong, the Lord made us this way. The only place we will find true safety and protection is in the care of Jesus. We often allow the fear of man to rob us from true security. If you believe you are safe by keeping an allegiance to someone outside of the Lord, it will always come with a price. He wants to set you free from the fear of man and the intimidation of the enemy.

I have years of personal experience of this. At times we shrink back and don't speak up for what we know is right, because we're afraid of the consequences. Every time we compromise, we give up part of who we truly are. We allow ourselves to be held in bondage, and sacrifice who God has truly called us to be. Don't give in to fear, don't give in to control. God has created you for freedom, for life and for truth. It takes courage to stand up and be strong, to say what you really think, and to hold fast to what you know God is leading you into. You are called to walk in the light, so don't partner with others in the darkness, gossiping behind people's backs. Don't be tempted to go along with the crowd, not honouring and loving the way you are called to. Don't be like these parents whose main concern was "being in" with the right crowd. Contrast their attempts to dodge the question, with the simple straightforward response from the son himself:

"Whether He (Jesus) is a sinner or not, I don't know. One thing I do know, I was blind but now I see!"
John 9:25

This man received his sight in the natural, but more importantly his eyes were opened to the spiritual truth that Jesus was the son of God. This is in stark contrast to the religious leaders, who John portrays as those who are truly blind ones. Ironically their legalism makes them reject God and they are incapable of seeing the truth. They are ignoring the words of the prophet Isaiah, who foretold that the Messiah would come and open the eyes of the blind, they are bad shepherds. They're the people who are abusing the sheep. They are the ones who are only interested in their own profit, their own advancement, their own reputation. This behaviour had been common throughout Israel's history, and had been warned about in the scriptures by the prophet Ezekiel:

"Son of man, prophesy against the shepherds of Israel;... Woe to you shepherds of Israel who only take care of yourselves!... You eat the curds, clothe yourselves with the wool and slaughter the choice animals, but you do not take care of the flock. You have not strengthened the weak or healed the sick or bound up the injured... You have ruled them harshly and brutally."
Ezekiel 34:2-4

Throughout scripture there were countless examples of bad shepherds who had abused the position of authority given to them by the Lord. Shepherds who had strayed away from God's path of love, justice, compassion and mercy. Jesus comes to confront this abuse of power and to show us what His Father is really like.

The gatekeeper

The images Jesus uses are very simple for us to understand. Shepherds were a very normal part of Jewish life. They would have been seen on the hills surrounding Jerusalem, and the sheep being called in by their shepherds at night was a common sight. Maybe as Jesus began His discourse, this actual scene was happening in the background. No one knows for certain, but we do know that everyone would have been familiar with the illustration He used.

Let's look at John 10, verses 1-3:

"Very truly I tell you Pharisees, anyone who does not enter the sheep pen by the gate, but climbs in by some other way, is a thief and a robber. The one who enters by the gate is the shepherd of the sheep. The gatekeeper opens the gate for him"

As we are not all familiar with farming practices at that time, reading this may not initially make much sense.

What does the gate and the gatekeeper mean? Every night people would have heard the shepherds calling their flocks off the plains for the night, gathering them into their folds for safety. They would have been intermingled through the day, so as each shepherd called out to his particular flock, the sheep would have listened for their own shepherds' call. His voice would have been familiar to them, and they would have followed him. They did not follow a different shepherd. You can see this still today. The gatekeeper would have looked after the folds and only permitted the shepherds he knew to bring in their sheep. He would have opened the gate, allowing them to bring in their flock. Then the sheep would have been safe for the night.

Jesus uses this illustration to expose the religious authorities and their treatment of the blind man. They are the thieves and robbers in His analogy. These leaders had driven the blind man out of the Jewish fold and Jesus explains that they had no authority to do so, they are bad shepherds. They're not concerned with the safety and welfare of those that they have been entrusted with.

Jesus explains that He is the only gate, and His Father is the gatekeeper. There's no other access to the Father other than coming through Him. By believing in Him, you come into the true fold. Here you find safety, protection, provision and comfort. He is the only way to become one of God's own flock. No position in society, or rule keeping, will get you access to the Father. Only trust and belief in the Son will.

Jesus is a different shepherd

Have you ever been made to feel like you're on the outside? Have you imagined that something from your past, or perhaps the generations before you, has excluded you from entering into a relationship of blessing and favour with God? Look who Jesus is reaching out to here. Those who had been rejected, the downtrodden, the outsiders, the undesirables. They find themselves being welcomed into the fold by Jesus. He deals with the rules and regulations that have disqualified them and shows what a good shepherd looked like. The religious leaders made God appear distant, cold and harsh. Life had been reduced to a transactional process of obeying rules and following laws. It placed a heavy burden that was too much to carry.

This simple truth is much the same for us. We deal with the same feeling of not being good enough. It's a fear that you don't meet the standard. Have you ever felt trapped in a cycle of defeat, searching for a way out, but not being able to find it? Jesus knows the burdens that weigh us down, and He wants us to live free from them:

"When He saw the crowds, He had compassion for them, because they were harassed and helpless, like sheep without a shepherd."
Matthew 9:36

Jesus does not only see your sin or your failure, He sees you through a different lens! He looks at who He has made you to be. He does not define you by your behaviour. He sees the potential placed within you and each day He is calling that out of you. There's a massive contrast here. What does a good shepherd then look like? When Jesus sees you He doesn't feel anger, disappointment or any other negative emotion. He is full of compassion.

You can hear His voice

"the sheep listen to His voice. He calls His own sheep by name and leads them out. When He has brought out all His own, He goes on ahead of them, and His sheep follow Him because they know His voice."
John 10:2-3

You are made for intimate connection with Jesus, and part of that means you can hear and recognise His voice. Unless you're a sheep farmer, you probably won't appreciate the significance of these words. The picture Jesus paints is a very familiar one for the people, they would have understood instinctively the relationship between the shepherd and the sheep. Earlier I talked about how the sheep would have recognised the unique call of their shepherd. They were tuned in to the sound of their shepherds voice, and would not respond to another call. The religious leaders were trying to destroy Jesus' credibility by trying to repute his heritage, and where His authority came from. However they were not able to deceive the people, as they were drawn to the voice of the true shepherd.

Mirror that with your own relationship with the Lord: we need to trust more that we hear the Lord speaking to us. We have made it so complicated and difficult, but that's not God's way. In fact, we have all been designed to recognise the voice of the Lord. There is part of us that instinctively knows when He is speaking to us. Many people wonder if God speaks to them like He does to others. It doesn't say here that the shepherd speaks to some of the sheep. It is simply not true that only a special few are chosen, and only they can hear His voice. It says the sheep listen to His voice, and that means all of them.

You are not excluded. We can all hear the voice of the shepherd. Sometimes we have bought into the lie that it couldn't be Him speaking to us. We allow fear and doubt to be the louder voice. We believe that we are not worthy, or do not qualify, but that is not the truth. God calls you personally. Notice that Jesus doesn't talk about how the shepherd deals with the flock. He talks about each individual sheep. He talks about a personal, intimate knowledge of those who He cares for. You have been built for connection with Jesus, you hear His voice and He calls you by name.

Remember when the shepherds were out on the hills there were many flocks together but they only responded to the voice of one. In your life there will be many voices calling for your attention, though only one of them will fully know you, and only one will bring true life.

He knows you completely

What else do we know about this intimate connection that Jesus wants to reveal through this image of the good shepherd?

> *"I know my sheep and my sheep know me, just as the Father knows me and*
> *I know the Father."*
> *John 10:14-15*

We are terrified at the thought of being really known. What would happen if the world was exposed to the unvarnished version of you, as opposed to the carefully managed image that we put out there? Here's the truth - you are fully known by Jesus. In the Old Testament, God had been revealed as the great I AM, as the Lord Almighty, the supreme God. He was all powerful and all knowing. He was mighty and He was just. These important attributes help us to understand who God is. Jesus came to show the greatest revelation of who God is. He reveals Him as Abba: Father.

This would have blown the minds of the Jews in Jesus' time. To them, God was far off and could never be approached. Strict rules and regulations governed who could draw close to God, and your name was unlikely to be on the guest list. The thought of God as a Father who was personal was too much. Jesus was removing all the barriers. He goes on to compare this intimate relationship between the sheep and the shepherd, with the intimacy between the son and the Father. This idea of being truly known is a deep need that lies in the heart of every man and woman. For someone to know us completely, but not reject us. To love us warts and all.

Jesus the good shepherd will lead and guide you

When someone knows us completely, we can have confidence in how they will lead us. It means they know exactly what we need. This is why the shepherd goes ahead and the sheep follow. It is a picture of complete trust, the sheep do not question where they are led, they follow willingly because they have such devotion and trust in the shepherd.

How many people are looking to be led through the challenges of life? How many people are facing uncertain times where the road ahead is unclear? The places where we have looked for provision are drying up, pastures we have gone to are no longer good feeding ground. So many people are looking for direction and safety. You do not need to worry or be anxious about your needs being met, Jesus, the good shepherd, is nurturing and leading you. This picture had been spoken of through the Prophet Isaiah:

"He will tend his flock like a shepherd; He will gather the lambs in his arms;
He will carry them in his bosom, and gently lead those that are with young."
Isaiah 40:11

Jesus is committed to helping you become everything that He has created you to be. This life is not about just surviving or getting through, it's a life of rest and fullness, and there is more! The sheep come in and go out, they can explore and move to new places; this isn't a life of restriction and confinement, it's a life of adventure and opportunity:

"The thief comes only to steal and kill and destroy; I have come that they
may have life and have it to the full."
John 10:10

How are you feeling as you read this? Are you excited about the opportunity that you have with the Lord or are you struggling? Are you feeling overwhelmed by demands? Do you feel like life is being stolen from you? Are you being robbed of precious time with your family? You might feel like an important relationship has been destroyed. It might be that some areas of your life feel dead and barren. The good news today is that Jesus, your good shepherd, cares for you. He knows you by name, He calls you His own, He has come to lead you into fullness.

Jesus is your protection

I went through through a phase of being terrified of getting onto a plane unless I had "pleaded" the blood of Jesus, and prayed for protection over every inch of the journey. It was crazy. I had listened to some well meaning preacher tell me that, unless I prayed every single time, the Lord would remove His hand of protection. At the same time His angels would turn a blind eye to whatever I was doing. I was a sitting duck. Talk about faith building! I now know that everything is taken care of, because my family and I are under the protective watch of the good shepherd. Jesus assures us that His commitment to our protection is not temporal and it cannot be revoked. He shows us the difference between the good shepherd and a hired hand. The loyalty of a hired hand can be bought and sold, they won't make the ultimate sacrifice in the face of danger. The good shepherd will sacrifice Himself for His sheep. The reason we can enjoy the fullness of life that God intends for us, is because of the price the shepherd was willing to pay, we can enjoy freedom from fear, and a life of wholeness, because Jesus has poured out His life on our behalf. Think of all those things that hold you back. All the things you are anxious about that take up your time and energy, leaving you tired and depleted. You have been set free from every one because Jesus voluntarily laid down His life for you.

Many of us have had times in our lives when we have put our faith in the wrong things. We have trusted in people, rather than trusting in the Lord. We have trusted in our own efforts. We have put our faith in the system of the world, relying on our employers, our education, our reputation and our connections. We hope that these things will provide the security and protection we crave, but like the hired hand, they can never be counted on. Anything outside of Jesus will leave you exposed to danger. Jesus points the Jews towards the sacrifice that He would make to save His people. This act of love He does in obedience to the will of the Father:

"The reason my Father loves me is that I lay down my life—only to take it up again. No one takes it from me, but I lay it down of my own accord. I have authority to lay it down and authority to take it up again. This command I received from my Father."
John 10:17-18

This total submission to the will of the Father is what brings you and I into freedom today. In laying down His life, He actually found it. By letting go and giving up His rights, He entered into the true purpose of His calling, and fulfilled His destiny. Surrendering His authority released Him into the highest place of blessing, and promoted Him to the highest honour- seated at His Father's right hand where every power has to bow the knee. Submission in the eyes of the world will never make sense. The religious leaders were clutching to the power they had seized, not knowing that if they had shown humility they would have got what they needed.

This is true for us today. How many times do we worry about what other people do? Those who try to bring you down. The voices that rise up against you. Jesus is above it all. He has every moment of your life in His hand, so you can trust 100 percent in His protection. He will go before you, He will lead you out. He watches over you, so you do not need to live in fear.

Jesus' work in you is way better than what you expect

The Jews had a clear view of what they thought they needed. They wanted the Romans gone, and an end to the oppression they represented. They were looking for a Messiah who would rescue them and protect them from their enemies. Jesus showed them that life with God was way beyond just the physical, outside world. His was a much deeper and richer work. This was not a quick fix, but a revolution of a totally different kind:

"I give them eternal life, and they shall never perish; no one will snatch them out of my hand. My Father, who has given them to me, is greater than all; no one can snatch them out of my Father's hand. I and the Father are one."
John 10:27-30

Many people today are trying to hold on and get through. In a world where nothing feels secure or certain, they are clutching at straws, giving themselves to whatever will create a sense of peace and security. You don't need to worry about these things. You are called for better than that. You are so important to Abba; He is holding you. There are many times when everything in life feels shaky and uncertain. When we feel like we are falling, we need to remind ourselves of the truth. No matter how we might feel, we are absolutely secure. We have hope. We have eternal safety. This reality is not based on our emotions, but based on the promises of God. We need a revelation of this every day. No earthly plan, scheme of the enemy, economic downturn or deadly disease can successfully come against the work of Jesus in your life. You are safe today and you have nothing to fear. More importantly, you do not need to fight to hold on. Don't think that you need to hold onto God. He is always holding onto you, and He will never let you go. Simply follow the voice of your good shepherd.

He will lead you to the right place at the right time. He will get you to those wide open spaces. He will open the doors for your promotion. He is always one step ahead, protecting you from all danger. He will never abandon you, leave you, or forsake you. He calls you his own. He knows you by name. He has laid down his life for you.

Jesus is your good shepherd!

12

Resurrection

"Did I not say believe and you would see?"
John 11:40

When people ask you something interesting about yourself what do you say? This happens in those really awkward "getting to know you" social scenarios which I find pretty uncomfortable. I've a couple of great facts about myself that people don't believe. Here's the first one, Penny and I got engaged after our final year of university when we were working at a summer camp in the US. I'd planned an amazing engagement moment, but it all nearly went wrong. I had a family connection to the US Secret Service and planned to pop the question whilst visiting the White House. This was in the mid 1990s' when the security situation was much different to what it is today. We were vetted for access to the private area of the West Wing, and I planned with my cousin how it was all going to happen. Penny had no idea. This sort of thing takes time to put in place, so I had to be really organised.

We had talked about getting married, and Penny asked me to help me choose her engagement ring. We bought the ring but the date we were given for the White House was still a couple of weeks away, so I would have to wait for the big moment. Penny did not have any idea what I was planning. As far as she was concerned I had the ring, and at any moment I would be down on one knee proposing. However, she had to wait, and then wait some more. When the day finally came, I organised for us to go sightseeing around Washington DC before our allotted time later that evening. By this stage though, Penny had had enough. Weeks had passed from buying the ring, and she thought I had changed my mind on the whole marriage idea, the day was a disaster.

Penny is not huffy or moody, but she was genuinely upset. She hardly spoke a word as I tried my best to fill hours of the most awkward sightseeing day ever. Finally, she burst into tears and said we needed to talk. That's never a great thing to hear as it's rarely good news. The day was quickly going up in flames. Question after question followed as I tried my level best to reassure her that I did love her, and had not changed my mind. She did not seem to believe me. To cut a long story short, we made it to the White House later that afternoon. We spent a couple of hours visiting and looking around which was fascinating. The press room was my favourite! And then, with a burly agent standing a few feet away, we found ourselves in a small ante room to the Oval Office, where I was able to propose. Thank goodness she said yes. What a difference a moment can make. The waiting nearly derailed what was supposed to be an incredible moment, but thankfully it did not.

The most incredible story

I think that I could write an entire book on this next portrait of Jesus. Every single person alive will be able to identify with much of what happens. This is the story of Lazarus, a friend of Jesus who dies, and then is raised from the dead. It's a story packed with meaning on many levels. We learn powerful truths about who He is and what He has done. It calls us to believe for more in our own lives. It causes faith to rise in us that no matter what weapons have been formed against us, if we will believe, we will see God's grace deliver us to victory.

The story is right in the middle of John's gospel. It separates the book and sets up the second half that is all about the journey that Jesus takes to the cross. This story is also a picture of what Jesus Himself will do. We see how He will die and yet be raised again. There are strong echoes of His own journey as we get to this point in the gospel narrative. For us this is all about hope. It's a story that speaks to the complex mix of challenges, fears, disappointments, confusion, hope and dreams that co-exist in all of us. It's for those who still hope that we will see better days, despite the challenges and questions. It's for those who refuse to give up. For those who say that I may not understand it, and at times I may not feel it, but Lord I still want to believe.

He doesn't fit your view

It's important to see how the story unfolds and what is going on in the background. Jesus has so incensed the Jews that they are now wanting to kill Him for blasphemy. As a result, He left Jerusalem. Lazarus is the brother of Mary and Martha. They appear in another famous story where Mary anoints the feet of Jesus, but that story has not yet happened. They live in Bethany, which in modern day Israel is an Arab town called El-Azariya. This name translated means "the place of Lazarus." It is found on the south eastern slopes of the Mount of Olives, about two miles from Jerusalem.

Let me summarise this first part. Jesus hears that His friend Lazarus is ill. Despite the disciples' urging, Jesus does not rush to his side, but waits two days before heading for Bethany, the home of Lazarus and his two sisters Martha and Mary. When Jesus finally decides to go to Bethany, the disciples urge caution because it is near Jerusalem, where there is a danger to Jesus' life.

Jesus hears that *"Lazarus is sick"* (John 11:3). What is your expectation of God whenever you know that God knows about your problem? Most of us want it sorted, and we can get impatient about it. We want it fixed and there is nothing wrong with that. It is perfectly normal when things are going wrong, to want to be delivered from them, that is why we go to the doctor when we are sick. We are built to be whole. Jesus then says:

> *"this sickness is not unto death"*
> *John 11:4*

When He looks at the same situation that you are looking at, He rarely comes to the same conclusion that you do. His view is different. He is God, and you are not. He has a different lens. Written into this statement from Jesus is a promise of deliverance from the very start. *"Not unto death."* We get very wrapped up in the apparent seriousness of our situation, and Jesus sees it entirely differently. He sees hope, completeness, promise and restoration, even when we do not. It feels like a disaster to us and He is saying "nah... I've got this.. I am going to show you heaven's power here." He is always setting you up for greater glory, to experience grace upon grace.

We read, *"He loved them"* (John 11:5). Everything that Jesus does in our lives starts and ends in His love for us. There is no other lens. He is only ever operating from a place of deep love and compassion towards us. Why do we need to remind ourselves of that? Our situations and circumstances will cause us to believe differently if we view them outside of the process of promise. We hope for deliverance, but we live with the tension of what we see and feel in the natural. In those times, our trust in the loving grace of Jesus can be undermined. Emotions can be strong and dominate large parts of our day. When trust in the Lord is undermined, we lose hope. This is why I love grace, because it is the unvarnished truth of the good news, all the time. For God so loved the world. He is only ever motivated by love for you.

Jesus doesn't always meet your expectation

If you didn't know this story what would you have expected Jesus to do? When you are facing your problems, what expectation of God do you have? Does Jesus hear about the situation and immediately run there as they expected him to do? No, He does not. He stays where He is and waits for another two days (John 11:6). He does not do things that we expect all the time, and that is where we must know, above all, that He only ever acts from love. The promise is that even when I cannot see it, He is operating in love towards me. This truth brings me to a place of faith and trust. This process can be difficult for us. When our understanding runs out and we stand stripped of anything we can do ourselves, the best option is to throw ourselves on the grace of God.

The disciples are also trying to work out what is going on. They ask *"are you going there?"* (John 11:8) This is the start of the great journey that Jesus will take towards His own death. He is going to be close to Jerusalem where some people are wanting to kill him. He is going to a place of personal danger, for Lazarus, the one He loves. The imagery is striking; in order for Jesus to save the ones He loves, He must go and give up His own life. He travels towards that place and not away from it. Jesus has a bigger view, and the bigger plan in mind. He will go to a place where He surrenders His life in order to save us.

The more impossible it is the bigger your miracle will be

On His way, Jesus is met by Martha, who heard that He was coming. She rushes to meet Him and reveals that Lazarus has died, and has been in the tomb four days. She says:

> *'Lord, if you had been here, my brother would not have died,*
> *but even now I know that God will grant whatever you ask of him'*
> *John 11:21*

Jesus promises her that her brother will rise again, but makes no promise that it will be now, rather than in the afterlife. In response, Martha affirms her belief that Jesus is:

> *'the Christ, the Son of God, the one who was to come into this world'*
> *John 11:27*

We see two different responses here that help us with how we respond in our challenges. At this point her brother has been dead for four days. I will come onto that, but there is no doubting that He is properly dead. I can identify with Martha as she runs out to meet Jesus:

> *"Lord, if You had been here, my brother would not have died. But even now*
> *I know that whatever You ask of God, God will give You."*
> *John 11:21-22*

Martha processes her angst and disappointment at the situation frankly. She can hardly hide her frustration with Jesus. How often do you do that? If truth be told, if you were not afraid of anything, what would you really want to say to Jesus about what has happened in your life, or about what is going on now? I see this in me - It's a bit Jekyll and Hyde to use that term. "I'm afraid, I'm frustrated, I know you love me and I know what your Word says, but it all just feels messed up right now." This is the sense I get from her.

Jesus replies with a straight promise:

"Your brother will rise"
John 11:23

Jesus is unequivocal. This is a hope filled, future building, life bringing declaration, in the middle of a situation that looks dead and lost. In every bit of processing, wondering and questioning that we do, Jesus replies to us with a promise of grace.

We are just like Martha. She is just not getting it. She says she understands about the resurrection on the last day, but what does that really mean? This is like us today saying "yeah I know that when we die and go to heaven it will all be okay." There is a vagueness about her reply, a lack of clarity and assurance. It's like "Yes I've heard that, I know this in my head, but it's not where I am at right now."

What does the Lord do when He sees that she is wobbling? Does He chastise her and tell her that she should know better? Does He shame her? No! He comes again with another faith declaration to her unsteadiness:

"I am the resurrection and the life... Do you believe?"
John 11:25

I love this. Can you hear Him saying this to you right now about your situation? Listen as He reassures you that whatever your problem is, no matter how big, impossible, insurmountable or discouraging it may appear, it is no bigger than death itself! This is not some vague hope for the future. It is a declaration of truth, that Jesus is bigger than anything you are facing. He says I have conquered it, and if you will believe, you will have my grace right now, transforming you in this moment. What are you believing for? Are you like Martha here? I am a lot. I live in the tension of what I see with my natural eyes, and what I know to be true -that He is greater than it all. Still though there is the tension.

When you just don't have it in you

Mary is different, and how the Lord responds to her is a magnificent display of grace:

"Then, when Mary came where Jesus was, and saw Him, she fell down at His feet, saying to Him, "Lord, if You had been here, my brother would not have died."
John 11:32

There is no massive display of faith here from Mary. Her response is different to that of her sister. She just falls at His feet. Mary will do that again later, not from a place of anguish, but from a place of adoration, when she anoints His feet with oil. I guess the point is found a couple of verses down. What does He do with us, when like Mary here, He sees us at our weakest? We read:

"Jesus wept"
John 11:35

He is not distant and unaware of how difficult your situation is. Do you notice what He did here? Mary had nothing but disappointment, however He didn't chastise her. He didn't tell her off, or lecture her on where she should be doing better. He didn't point the finger. You might feel like the only place you want to fall is at the feet of Jesus, and there be honest that you have nothing to bring. He loves that. That is a place where His grace can truly flow to you. Empty of yourself, empty of your own effort, with nothing left to try. In that place she really touched the heart of Jesus, and so He wept.

He is full of love for you. He is not distant and without feeling for you. He is moved by what is going on with you right now. He knows, He understands, He sees and He doesn't judge you. When we are at our lowest point religion will tell us that we have failed and that we should be better. Religion accuses us, saying at this stage of our lives we should know better. We fear that things will never change, that we are not as loved as someone else. The real truth is that when we feel weakest and most empty, as scary as that place can be, we are in the very best place to receive what we need from the Lord.

It all turns around

There are some brilliant details that add more depth to the story. On reaching Lazarus' tomb, despite Martha's protests that after four days the smell of Lazarus' body will be overwhelming, Jesus commands the stone be removed. He calls Lazarus to come out of the tomb. At Jesus' word, still bound by his burial cloths, Lazarus comes out. Just a moment before he was undoubtedly dead. Jesus tells the onlookers to unbind Him and let him go free from the captivity of death.

Can you imagine being there? Like my day in Washington, it seems like victory is being snatched from the jaws of defeat. We don't know the cause of Lazarus' death, but we do know he was in the tomb, stone dead, for four days. To the witnesses at Bethany, his raising was absolutely miraculous. Even more so as the Jewish understanding was that the soul lingered with the corpse for three days, only leaving when the body burst open. That is pretty gross!

What must it have been like in that tomb with Lazarus? Upon his death, his body would have been washed, wrapped in burial cloths, and anointed with oils. After four days his body would have started to decompose, and the tomb, a cave in which Lazarus' body had been laid, would have begun to smell horribly of the stench of death. Literally his body would decay and break apart.

The Jews viewed Lazarus' body as ritually unclean, and not to be touched under any circumstances. Not only would the stench of Lazarus' decaying body have been present in the tomb but as there was a huge stone in front of the entrance, no light would have penetrated the space leaving it in total darkness. This place was the absolute embodiment of death, and there was no way that any person was escaping it. Remember, this is a picture of what Jesus Himself is going to do. It is a demonstration of the power of Jesus to defeat death and all of its' effects.

The law reversed

We tend to think about physical death when we read this story. We have to remember all of the promises about Messiah through the Gospel of John and the prophecies that they echo. This is another example where we see a rich tapestry, full of depth and meaning. There was no light in the tomb because the stone was in front of it. This is a picture of the written law:

"who also made us sufficient as ministers of the new covenant, not of the

letter but of the Spirit; for the letter kills, but the Spirit gives life"
2 Corinthians 3:6

The law was written on tablets of stone. Jesus uses the metaphor of the tomb, and the stone, to show how the law stops the light of God's grace from bringing life. It keeps people in darkness and it stinks, our inability to keep the law perfectly results in death.

What does Jesus do? He declares:

"Roll away the stone"
John 11:38

Let me paraphrase so we see exactly what is going on. This is grace Himself prophetically declaring that He will "roll away" the written law, with all its' demands, all of its' burdens, all of its' penalties. He will roll it away so that light may come to the darkest, most stinking place of your life. As the light of His love and grace touches the innermost part of you, it is not for shame and punishment but only so that His healing may flow. Whatever is dead comes alive as the power of grace transforms impossible situations.

We are Martha

Martha's reaction is one of the most honest moments I see in this whole story. It helps me, because not only do I see myself in it, but the way in which Jesus responds to her is amazing. What does she say? I imagine her being confronted with the facts. Her brother is very dead, and so she asks Jesus, "Are you sure about this? You're telling these guys to take away the stone?" Just to make sure Jesus really understands the situation she says:

"Lord, by this time there is a stench, for he has been dead four days."
John 11:40

This is fantastic. This is why there is no other gospel, and no other truth other than unmerited favour, the gospel of grace. Martha doesn't think that grace will be enough, she doubts. So she says to Jesus "Really? Do you know he's completely dead?"

The apostle Paul wrote that we should never allow anyone to lead us a different gospel. How ludicrous is it, that we have people today who say that you need to be careful with grace. What they are in fact saying is that grace is not enough. They say you need something more than grace through faith alone.

How are you looking at challenges in your own life and in others? So often in the face of those things that we know we are powerless to change, we still have this crisis of confidence saying, "Lord are you sure? Is your promise of grace enough?" There is absolutely nothing that anyone can do here. Lazarus is four days dead. All natural options have run out. They are only faced with impossibility and yet she questions "Lord do you really understand what is happening here?"

How often do we convince ourselves that we have something to offer and to bring? How does Jesus respond?

"Did I not say believe and you would see?..... Did I not say believe?"
John 11:40

You might be at a place right now where you are staring impossibility in the face, and you know that you have nothing to give. You may have heard the promise of grace many times and are still not sure that it is enough. I am amazed at how many times I find myself in that situation. Though I know I cannot do it, I still doubt that He will. Our crisis of faith in these moments is that we cannot see, when faced with impossibility, that grace is enough. What does the Lord say to you in those moments? I hear the words of Paul when he said:

"My grace is sufficient for you, for my power is made perfect in weakness. Therefore I will boast all the more gladly about my weaknesses, so that Christ's power may rest on me."
2 Corinthians 12:9

I love what the Lord does here: He does not come down to the level of our unbelief, but instead He shows us that He is true to every promise. It is impossible for Him to lie. He backs up His words with a demonstration of His power.

Jesus lifted up *"His eyes,"* echoing the writer in Psalm 121:1, *"I lift up my eyes... where does my help come from?"* and said, *"Father, I thank You that You have heard Me."* No matter how dark it is, your declaration of praise will shift you to a place of grace and open up your world for a miracle. Jesus then said. **"And I know that You always hear Me".** *He cried with a loud voice, "Lazarus, come forth!"* (John 11:41-43).

And then the miracle happened:

"And he who had died came out bound hand and foot with grave clothes, and his face was wrapped with a cloth. Jesus said to them, "Loose him, and let him go."
John 11:44

There we have it. Death itself is no match for the King of Grace. Whatever is going on in your life right now, it's no match for the power of Jesus. The dead come to life, death is defeated, and life bursts out from every place of decay. That is grace. We don't need to have it all together, like some sort of spiritual super hero. Jesus loves you. Jesus is working out greater glory in your life than what you could ever imagine. When you cannot see it, like Penny that day in Washington, don't allow the disappointment to steal the hope that His Word promises. This is what He is saying to you right now; in every situation, no matter what it is, our only response needs to be faith in what grace can do. He has already shown that He is greater than even our biggest enemy; death itself.

"I am the resurrection and the life." When grace collides with death there is only ever one outcome. And that is life!

13

What is true?

"I am the way and the truth and the life... No one comes to the Father except through me"
John 14:6

When I was a kid I used to love a TV programme called 'Tomorrow's World.' It was made by the BBC and was all about looking into the future to see how technology was going to transform life as we knew it. I remember being fascinated by what seemed to be the most outlandish advances in everything, from transport to devices for the home. This was the first time I saw a music CD and I was nearly floored. Up until this point I had suffered the pain of many cassette tapes unravelling, then trying my best to wind the tape back together with a pencil. There is somebody reading this and you do not have the first clue what I am talking about, but others have been there and understand completely. The sense of panic as your favourite mix tape unwound around the player is something that scarred a generation. I remember showing my son Ben a cassette when he was younger and asking him if he knew what it was. He just looked at me like I had walked off the ark. He couldn't believe that we had been so backward, that he said he felt sorry for me.

There have been changes in our physical world in my lifetime that can only be described as incredible. We would not have believed what was possible even ten years ago. However, that is not the biggest change by any stretch of the imagination. There has been a much more profound change in the world that has more serious implications for every one of us. In fact sometimes when I engage with mainstream and social media, I can scarcely believe some of the changes that are happening.

Post-truth world

We are living in what has been described as a post-truth world. The Oxford definition of a post-truth society is one in which objective facts matter less than appeals to emotion. In *Saving Truth: Finding Meaning and Clarity in a Post-Truth World*, Abdu Murray does a great job of explaining what has happened over the last few decades. He says that we are living in a "culture of confusion." We elevate individual preferences over truth. We also elevate individual autonomy (freedom *from* constraints), over true freedom (freedom *within* constraints). Whereas autonomy is the freedom to make *any* choice according to preference, true freedom is making the *right* choice according to truth. I have seen this battle out now for years and it comes down to two opposing points of view; one is that facts do not care about your feelings, the other is that personal preference becomes truth. The idea of anything being objectively true is now out the window, and truth can be defined by whatever you feel it is. Fundamentally though, for anything to be considered true, it must be objective. If something is true, then it is true whether or not anyone believes it. These changes are an attempt to understand the world and our place within it. One of the challenges is that the world is not becoming more tolerant of different views. There is a new orthodoxy emerging, one that is more, and not less hostile of ideas that do not fit the "mainstream' narrative. This can be seen in increasing animosity towards Christians, who are painted as intolerant and out of touch.

Living in a post-truth world

There are many negative effects of living in a world where the notion of objective truth no longer applies. There is the erosion of trust, the undermining of authority and a growing lack of interest in evidence of any sort. In this context the next I am statement of Jesus seems to be completely outrageous:

"I am the way and the truth and the life. No one comes to the Father except through me"
John 14:6

If there is one way to open yourself up to abuse and criticism, it is to state that there is only one source of truth, and that you are it! Jesus goes further than that by saying there is no other way possible for human beings to get to God. When He said this it would have caused a massive problem for the religious leaders, who were building their hope for salvation on their ability to keep the demands of the law. That was how they felt they could reach God.

In our modern world the implications of Jesus' words are even more profound. One of the dangers that I see is the idea of truth being so personal and malleable it leads to a deep insecurity in people. If what I think, or feel, on any particular day is 'truth' then it would be reasonable to assume that human beings as a group would be on an upward curve of peace, security and wholeness. If every day was filled with truth, then our lives would reflect a higher state of existence. This is what Maslow described as a state of self actualisation. The experience of living in this world would only be better as each day unfolds. Why? Because we are all apparently becoming more enlightened as we live in truth.

The picture is somewhat different though, we have an epidemic of loneliness despite being the most "connected" generation in history. Rates of mental health issues such as depression, anxiety and suicide, especially among young people are growing exponentially. In listing many of the other challenges we face you will see the scale of the problem: pollution and the environment, inequality, low pay and poverty, unemployment and underemployment, race relations, crime, law and order, sexual inequalities, drug and alcohol abuse, the breakdown of the nuclear family and finally a lack of faith (trust) in government, politicians and the church.

Of course these are big and complex problems that require a huge investment of expertise to address; however how do we think that we can ever hope to solve them without some objective view of what is right and wrong? Perhaps some of these problems are made worse by the fact that we have abandoned any notion of what 'truth' means.

Is truth found in Jesus?

This is a bold claim, but the fact is that we all need an external point of reference in our lives, a north star if you like. We need something beyond ourselves that we point to, and from where we can take our bearings. I am a very stable person, but I know the battle that I can have with my emotions on a daily basis. If I was to build my life around my emotional state at any particular time, I would very easily find myself in deep trouble. For example, I have formed new opinions about people and subjects that are much different now to what they were ten years ago. How can both be true? How we think and feel is constantly changing.

I may at any point in time sincerely believe something and I may be sincerely wrong.

I don't have much spare time these days to play golf, but it used to be one of my most favourite things to do. In the big scheme of things I was absolutely below average in my ability, but I loved it nevertheless. Now I could truly believe and feel that I am as good as Rory McIlroy, but that thought alone does not make it so. As soon as that feeling is tested against an objective standard, i.e. Rory's statistics, the whole world can see that I am anything but another golfing prodigy, despite what I might believe.

What does Jesus have to say to us about this whole idea of what is true? He said that He Himself is the truth. The word that He used was *alithea*. Thayers Greek Lexicon defines this word as "*1 - objectively, 2 - universally,* **what is true in any matter under consideration** *(opposed to what is feigned, fictitious, false)*" Strong's concordance talks about "*reality as the opposite of illusion.*"

Jesus is making a huge statement that clashes with all the noise that surrounds us today. In a world of illusion masquerading as truth, He declares that He is divine truth revealed to mankind. He is the objective standard for all matters relating to life. His words and His life define and demonstrate truth for us, our job is not to create truth, but to discover it in the person of Jesus. In fact we will never know what truth is unless we first find it in who Jesus is, and what He has done. We do not need to be all at sea when it comes to the issues that we face today. In a world of billions of thoughts, feelings and opinions there is one that is above it all. The issue today is not that people have a problem with truth *per se*, but rather they do not like to hear truth that runs contrary to their own feelings.

Why would this matter to me anyway?

When there is no objective standard of truth then we will forever live insecurely. Jesus does not just make the statement that He is the truth just to be confrontational, there is a purpose for us to discover. He is linking back to a statement He made earlier in the book of John:

> *"You will know the truth and the truth will set you free"*
> John 8:32

The word here for knowing is a Greek word *ginosko* which means *"to know through personal, first hand experience."* This is the key for us, Jesus does not set Himself up in your life as just another source of teaching or wisdom, that sits equally with any other. I know to some that this may sound like a limiting statement, I mean why would it matter to you that Jesus is truth? This is the profound revelation that we miss. Jesus does not want you to simply have a head understanding of doctrine and truth, but rather He is inviting you to a life of grace that is to be lived and experienced. Experiencing His grace flowing in you will set you free. The word here is *eleutheróō* – which means *"properly, set free, release from bondage; (figuratively) to remove the restrictions of sin."* That is an amazing statement for the world today.

We have a culture that tells people freedom is found in self, and frankly it's just not working. I see a world that is more distracted, disjointed and reliant on medication, but still will not give it up and admit that we all need something more than humanity itself can provide. Jesus says what you are searching for you will find in me; I will help you see yourself for who you truly are. I will give you more hope, purpose and future than a million Instagram followers could ever do. I will heal your heart and make you secure. I will break the cycles of shame and guilt that plague you. I will give you peace, deal with your anxieties and give you a sound mind. That is what happens when we live in truth: we will no longer be pushed by every whim and ideology that is concocted by the latest influencer, but rather have our lives firmly established on the rock that will never be shaken.

Knowing truth brings you hope

There is another reason why this matters to us, it brings us hope. I have had many times in my life where circumstances were dire and I knew I was in a world of trouble, emotions ran high and despite really trying I could not see a way out. For example when Penny and I were seeing doctors about infertility, it felt like a black cloud had parked itself over our entire lives; we had little hope and needed a new perspective, which we found in the finished work of Jesus.

This is what happens whenever grace collides with your situation. Whatever the problem, it changes whenever you look at it through the lens of grace. We were in a hopeless situation. The "truth" according to medicine was that Penny and I would really struggle to conceive our own natural family. We learned to ask ourselves that very question - what does this situation look like when I examine it through the lens of Jesus and His finished work? How does it change? Jesus demonstrated many times that He is our healer, the Bible is full of accounts of Jesus encountering sickness and people being healed.

If we take the verses we have read in this chapter, we see how power-lessness becomes hope. I remember telling myself to believe that Jesus is our healer. If that revelation from the Bible is truth, then Jesus wants me to experience that first hand (ginosko) and be freed (*eleutheróō*) from sickness. That was our bold declaration even when we did not see anything change. Interestingly as we shifted our attention to a different, higher opinion of our situation, it caused hope to rise in us. We were no longer helpless, but we could say that we had a growing expectation of His goodness in our lives. We started to see what He desired for us. Truth shifts your heart and mind to a place of hope, a place where you can believe, that no matter what is going on in you or around you; there is a greater authority who has the final word on your life, that is the truth.

There will be many things that will try and set themselves up in your life in a place of authority. My encouragement to you is to prioritise what Jesus accomplished through His death and resurrection as the primary truth in your life, you will be anchored and restful when the challenges come. I don't think we need to shout and compete with all the other voices out there today; the Lord is simply saying; 'come to me, receive grace upon grace and you will be changed from the inside out.' The world will pay attention to that: not truth simply in words, but truth demonstrated in transformed lives.

14

The power of connection

"I am the vine, you are the branches. He who abides in Me, and I in him,
bears much fruit; for without Me you can do nothing."
John 15:5

Penny and I are, without doubt, the least talented people in the world when it comes to plants and gardening. This is not a recent phenomenon either. It's not that we don't enjoy the outside and appreciate a beautiful garden. We love the outdoors but have always been really bad at cultivating anything successfully, whether it's inside or outside. I remember times where people very kindly bought us a lovely house plant, and all I could think as they handed it over was "give this thing a couple of days and it'll be dead." Even when we follow the instructions, we cannot seem to get our plant game in any sort of proper order. My mum at one stage thought that she would try buying us one of those plants that needs next to nothing in terms of watering and feeding. Even that didn't make it past a couple of weeks. We have a gift of something, I'm just not sure what it is.

Ironically someone gifted a big indoor plant to our church before the COVID lockdown began, and it has grown to quite a size. I have affectionately named it the Triffid after the the fictional plant from the John Wyndham novel, that is able to move around and kill people with a poisonous stinger. I said to our team that it was getting too big and that we should stop looking after it. Despite my best efforts to finish this particular one off, it has absolutely flourished and grown even more. I set my sights on deliberately not trying with this plant, yet it has defied the odds. As we speak it is slowly but surely taking over the coffee lounge in our church building, and I have grown to really like it.

Are you tired?

The next portrait of Jesus has been very misunderstood for as long as I remember. It's been used to keep people in fear of getting things wrong. I imagine that people who taught like that were sincere in their view of what Jesus said, but I believe that they were sincerely wrong. Religion is exhausting, its demands are unbending and unrelenting. It tires us out, not just physically but also on a deeper emotional and spiritual level. If you know what that feels like then the words of Jesus will be like a drink of ice water on a roasting hot day. Grace at its very root brings us rest from trying to please God and our efforts to make ourselves better for Him. I have felt so tired under the weight of trying to do the right thing. I also see it as a pastor and leader in the people that we minister to. We have a heart to live for God, but we just can't pull it off on our own as it's too hard. We live in a cycle of perpetual defeat, lurching from one set of good intentions to another. Grace shows us a better way. Jesus has great news for you as you read this promise:

"Come to me, all who labour and are heavy laden, and I will give you rest."
Matthew 11:28

In the original words that Jesus uses, there is a revelation of grace that is deeply refreshing for weary souls. The word *kopiaó* means *to labour until you are worn-out, depleted (exhausted) in both a mental and physical way*. What does Jesus do when that is our state? Does He say that we just need to try harder? Not at all, He promises rest. The original word here is *anapaúō* which means *"to give and experience rest after the needed task is completed."* This is a great truth about the way that The Lord wants us to live. The work of provision for all that we need is already done. That is what we mean by 'a finished work.' And that work was not ours, it is His. The task of clearing the way for relationship with God is done already. There's nothing more that we can add to it. All of our efforts don't add one jot to what Jesus has already accomplished; we simply make ourselves tired and strengthen the very sin that we want to escape from. That does not make us lazy however. Grace is not opposed to activity, it is opposed to earning God's favour.

The vine

Jesus used an image that made perfect sense to His audience. On the front of the temple in Jerusalem was carved a golden vine to remind the people of the call that God had placed on them: Vines bear fruit and Israel was called to be a type of vine that would supply the life, knowledge and life of God to the surrounding nations. This was part of their calling. They were to be the most fruitful of all the nations, as an example of the blessing of God. God wanted the nations to see His goodness, kindness and favour through the nation of Israel, so they would be a demonstration of His power. We read:

"You brought a vine out of Egypt; you drove out the nations and planted it."
Psalm 80:8

We know they failed to do this. Repeatedly they were unable to fulfill any promise they made. As Jesus spoke they were bowed under the weight of Roman oppression and the demands of the religious system of law. In this context Jesus makes His declaration that He is the true vine:

"I am the true vine, and my Father is the vinedresser. Every branch in me that does not bear fruit He takes away, and every branch that does bear fruit He prunes, that it may bear more fruit. Already you are clean because of the word that I have spoken to you. Abide in me, and I in you. As the branch cannot bear fruit by itself, unless it abides in the vine, neither can you, unless you abide in me. I am the vine; you are the branches. Whoever abides in me and I in him, he it is that bears much fruit, for apart from me you can do nothing."
John 15:1-5

Not only would that have rocked the listeners of the day, but I believe that this message is one of the most needed truths that we have as modern believers. It is the crux of grace. It cuts right through all of our striving, and sets a rock solid foundation for living. The religious types would have been hugely offended at the notion that all of their work was powerless to produce even an ounce of godliness. The whole system was built with their effort at the centre. However for those who were, and still are, tired out by a never ending cycle of defeat, guilt and shame, this is the best news ever.

Binary truth

People get a little uncomfortable with the suggestion that something can be absolute. I remember a church leader telling me to be careful as there was no such thing as black and white. Our job as leaders, I was told, was to manage the grey. I understand that not everything in life is black and white, however there are some things that are distinct and they need to be. There is a binary that has huge implications for how we experience life. Jesus does not offer us grey, there is no scale of vine versus branch. Categorically He states that He is the vine and we are the branches, the distinction is crucial. The vine serves as the source and sustenance of life for the branches. A branch can only receive what comes to it through the vine. We have heard this said before, yet we still live like we are the vine. By that I mean we believe that we are the real source of all that we need. We know in our heads what these verses say, but we demonstrate what we really believe by how we live?

Have you seen where the fruit sits on a vine? It's on the branch. The vine and the branches are one, but there are two distinct roles if you like: the vine is where the life, water, food and all that is needed for fruit to grow comes from. It just so happens that this is passed through to the branches, and that is where the fruit is produced. This tells us that we are not the source of the fruit in our lives; our role is not one of producing but receiving. We bear good fruit whenever we are constantly receiving the grace of Jesus in our lives. When we constantly feed ourselves on grace, we bear good fruit.

The issue is that we get that mixed up: we live as though the results and the manifestation of fruitfulness are our responsibility. We may concede at times that it is the Lord that does it, but we think He needs some help from us along the way. We have to add to what Jesus has done. Why do we do that whenever Jesus is so clear? Why do we still try to take on responsibility for things that we simply have no hope of controlling? It robs us of rest in every part of who we are physically, spiritually and emotionally. A true branch is restful because it knows that all of its supply is coming from the vine.

Let's look at this picture a little bit more closely. It is interesting that the same life that flows in the vine is the same life that flows in the branch. Think about that: the life of Jesus is flowing through you right now! He is your source. He is your supply. It is His life, His power, His healing, His blessing and His hope that is flowing towards you at all times. This grace is the most powerful force in the universe and beyond; it is freely available to you.

So what do I do then?

You might be thinking that I must do something? Grace does not make us lazy and faith always requires a response, yet Jesus tells us that we are to "abide." This word is *Meno* and it simply means "*Stay, remain where you are.*" In other words stop trying to be something that you are not and could never be anyway. The sense is don't try to be a vine: you are a branch, so stay as a branch. Our response is to keep Jesus at the very centre of our heart and attention. This is a posture of deep trust that has ramifications for how we live. It means we do not try to be a supplier because we are not responsible for producing the fruit in our life. Every bit of it is a gift of God's grace. A true branch is restful and carefree because it knows that all the supply is coming from the vine and it trusts that the supply will produce the fruit. Grace does not elevate us based on how good or qualified we are, Grace elevates Jesus and points to His work as being the reason why we are blessed. That was the picture of the vine from the very start:

> "*But for this purpose I have raised you up, to show you my power,*
> *so that my name may be proclaimed in all the earth.*"
> *Exodus 9:16*

Your restfulness will be a greater testimony than your words. The more we learn the unforced rhythms of grace it seems the more fruitful and blessed we will be, that takes religious thinking and knocks it upside down!

Don't get in the way

So the more we rest, the more His supply flows to us. The opposite must also be true -when we resist grace, we cut off the life of God in us. Deep restfulness is not being lazy: it is as we live in the Spirit of God and allow Him to lead us that activity happens. However the results of the activity go far beyond what we could produce ourselves. So rest is not laziness, rest is the inner posture of trusting in His grace.

I live a very full and busy life and my days are often completely filled. Yet I am learning to live from the inside out, where activity is not exhausting. A place where all of what I do is as a response to what grace has done. It is not to 'win grace' - in fact the more we work the worse it is:

"You are severed from Christ, you who would be justified by the law; you have fallen away from grace."
Galatians 5:4

I used to think this is what happened when private failure became public, when someone got found out we would say that they had 'fallen from grace.' Falling suggests coming off high ground, but there is not one single verse in the New Testament that says when you sin that you fall out of God's grace. Falling from grace means that we go back under self effort and works; long before someone sins, they first fall from grace. We see that in the Old Testament; remember when the children of Israel proudly boasted at the foot of Mount Sinai that they would be able to keep whatever God commanded them to do? They fell at the first hurdle as they began to worship the golden calf. The fall from grace into self reliance and self effort is what brought about sin. Sinners had no problem receiving from Jesus, it was the self righteous and the Pharisees that could not receive from Him. Every sin we struggle with finds its root in trusting and relying on ourselves, and not trusting in grace.

Is God just really out to get me?

Whenever I meet someone who does not speak English I adopt the universal strategy of communication, it's not very effective and requires a fair bit of effort. It usually involves speaking more loudly, more slowly and waving my arms a lot. We miss out on so much when we do not know what the other person means or is trying to say. This happens frequently when it comes to translating the language of the Bible into English; really important things get lost in translation and we can miss the point.

The image of a vine is so loaded with meaning. To get the vine to be fruitful, it was placed on a trellis, which was normally a wooden cross type structure. The vine and the branches would intertwine together around the trellis; what a beautiful picture of the cross of Jesus. It is a picture of union and dependence. It also seems totally at odds with what Jesus says next:

> *"Every branch in me that does not bear fruit he takes away."*
> John 15:2

These verses terrified the life out of me growing up! The picture of God as an angry gardener waiting to cut me never really blessed me. This is teaching that says where there is sin in your life, God will cut us because that is good for us. It suggests that the only option the Lord has to get us to the place He wants us to be is through punishment. This creates a difficulty that can undermine my view of God.

I have so many questions like, how do we know how much fruit is enough before the secateurs are brought out? Is there a standard applied equally to us all that the Lord uses or are we left just guessing? How much fruit is enough? Will he demand more from me than someone else? What about if I am really trying but just a bit slower than someone else? No one has ever been able to answer this for me. If God is truly fair and just then there must be a standard that is applied equally to everyone. What is it and where can I find it? The result of this thinking means we have constant insecurity that we are not producing enough, in fact it puts the onus of fruit production right back on your shoulders, the real answer is much different.

The word for "takes away" is *Airo* and it means to *lift up;* when a vine is on the ground and in the dirt it cannot bear fruit. The muck and the dirt cover the leaves so they cannot receive light, the farmer must lift it up and wrap it around the trellis again. It is the same for us: when we are down and wallowing around in sin we cannot bear fruit. In viticulture, growers want to avoid any part of the cordon from touching the ground because of the vine's natural inclination to send out suckers or basal shoots and take root in that area where the cordon is touching the ground. This can lead to disease entering the plant; God does not want you to take root in the dust. This is a picture of feeding from the world, He does not want us to draw what we need from the wisdom of the world. So what does He do? Does He cut you to pieces? No! He lifts you up again to the cross, to the place of the finished work of Jesus where we can receive all that we need.

Pruned

"Every branch in me that does not bear fruit He takes away, and every branch that does bear fruit He prunes, that it may bear more fruit."
John 15:2-3

What goes through your mind when you hear the word prune? I think of cutting away, I imagine it to be a painful process of chastisement. In my limited knowledge of gardening I realise that is what happens with plants. Often parts of a tree are cut away because they are dead, broken or diseased. Is that what this verse means?

Grace is not a license to sin. I am a dad to three great kids and if there was something going on in their lives that was hurting them I would want it to stop. If they were giving themselves to something harmful then of course I would want to it end, that is not what is in question here. Jesus hates sin because of what it does to his children, the real question though is how does He get us out of it?

The word that is used here is not cut as we understand it, it is the word *kathiro* and its main meaning is to cleanse with water. This is so profound that it really rocked me when I first started to see it: in the middle eastern countryside of Jesus' day the vines would get dirty from insects, dust, dirt and moss. They became barriers to the leaves bearing fruit so the vine dresser washed the leaves clean with water so to remove the detritus. This is not cutting away but washing clean. We need to dig further here.

Jesus confirmed our position in verse 3:

"Already you are clean because of the word that I have spoken to you."
John 15:3

The word clean is *katharos* and it means *"clean, pure, unsoiled, to be ceremonially and morally clean."* Was Jesus confused here? Why would he be hacking away at something that was already unsoiled and morally clean? Religion tells us that before you meet Jesus you are a sinner and after you meet Jesus you are still a sinner, not much good news there for anybody! Grace tells us something entirely different. In Romans 3 we read:

"But now the righteousness of God has been revealed independently
and altogether apart from the Law."
Romans 3:21

This is so clear, to be righteous (Greek *dikaiousne*) means *"a condition approved and acceptable to God"* and *"What is deemed right / approved in His eyes after examination."*

So only after you have received Jesus we see:

"[All] are justified and made upright and in right standing with God, freely
and gratuitously by His grace (His unmerited favour and mercy), through
the redemption which is [provided] in Christ Jesus"
Romans 3:24

The word redemption here means *"buying back from, re-purchasing that which was previously lost. The emphasis is on the distance [safety margin] that results between the rescued person and what previously enslaved them."*

This is very simple. Whenever you received Jesus He made you totally acceptable and gave you right standing with God; you are no longer judged for your sin. There is a distance between who you were and who you are now. However, we still do mess it up so what happens then? How does Jesus cleanse us from bitterness, jealousy, fear, unforgiveness, hatred, impatience and all of the other stuff that we get involved in? He does it by the washing of His word.

When you sit under the word of grace it lifts you up again and then you will bear more fruit in your life. The Word shows us what Jesus' work has done for us. We need to be continually mindful of that. When we first received Jesus He *"perfected us forever"* (Hebrews 10:14) and from that place we are being changed from glory to glory as we mature in the faith and grow in grace. He promised us that He who began a good work in us the moment we were saved by grace through faith, will continue to transform our new born-again life in Christ, into the image and likeness of Himself.

He cleanses us not through punishment but by lifting us up again to that place where we see Jesus; that place where we receive His love. The more that you hear about Jesus and His love for you the more fruit you will see, that is why I so believe in the gospel of grace.

Wash your feet

I do love the character of Peter. He was so full on in everything that I imagine He would have been a handful to be around. I love that we see the ability to walk with Jesus and mess it up so badly all happening at the same time, his story gives me hope. In John 13 we watch as Jesus is washing the disciples feet in the upper room. This seemed like an odd thing to do and there are many ways that we can apply it. For example how we should serve each other and lay our lives down for one another.

That is absolutely true though I think that when seen in the context of Jesus' words in John 15 we get a much more profound truth. Peter here goes for it and says he wants his head and his hands washed as well. The feet are not enough for him.

In John 13:10, Jesus says to him, *"The one who has bathed (Louo - literally and metaphorically) – i.e. a complete bathing to cleanse the entire person does not need to wash, except for his feet, but is completely clean)... And you are clean"* (*Katharos - either literally or ceremonially or spiritually; guiltless, innocent, upright*).

Is Jesus being cryptic again or what did He mean? Why would Jesus say that you only need to wash your feet? He is saying that you are indeed made clean entirely by His work. We are not trying to be clean, we are already clean. When He saved you it was complete, total and whole. In a moment you were changed forever; you are spiritually guiltless and upright. Jesus says that when you have been cleansed like that you don't need to be cleansed again and again. Our feet are just the picture of where we touch the earth. A picture of where we connect with this world that we live in. We do have to walk through mess, we get ourselves into places that we should not be in. We get covered in the stuff of life at times and it sticks to us. Our feet get dirty.

So what do we do? Where we feel sullied and tainted by sin we go to the word of grace and let it wash us again. We let it pour over us and remind us that we are righteous and in right standing with God. As His children we can never forfeit His presence. The word will wash away disappointment, anxiety, fear and everything else that condemns us and shames us. We do not need to get saved all over again when we mess it up. We need to go to Jesus and allow Him to wash us with His words of grace. This is how you will bear much fruit. We get messy and life affects us all, we make mistakes and let ourselves and others down. When that happens, rest and go to grace. You will soon feel clean, refreshed and ready to go again. In fact at your very moment of failure the best thing that you can do is to declare the truth of your righteousness. Remind yourself that Jesus did a work in you and your failure does not change your standing with Him.

Rest and allow Him to work

In the time taken to write this chapter I have walked past the Triffid in our coffee lounge probably a dozen times. It is still there doing its thing. I went over to see how it was doing up close and amazingly it seems to be going from strength to strength. I have a feeling that someone has been secretly watering it. It is still there, planted deep, drinking water and growing a little day by day. It reminds me of what we should be like. Pastor Joseph Prince said that when we rest the Lord is able to work on our behalf. But if we choose to work, then the Lord rests. I hope that you are encouraged that Jesus is your vine, you can rest in His promise to supply all that you need for each and every day. You cannot work for that which is given as a gift. Rather we simply get planted deep in His love for us and from that place trust that the good fruit we need will come.

15

Famous last words

Late night googling can be dangerous. I have often found myself looking for a simple piece of information and before I know it I've disappeared down a Wiki rabbit hole that ends up with articles about nuclear fission, or some other random topic. It's just too easy to click those links. When I was preparing the sermon series that this book is based on, I found myself doing the same thing again. I cannot quite remember how I got there, but I ended up reading a list of the last words of famous people before they died. I would love to think that when it comes to my turn I will have my family gathered around me as I dispense my last words of wisdom, leaving them a poignant reminder of who I am.

It doesn't work out like that for everyone though. For example John Sedgwick, General of the Union Army during the US Civil War said, "They couldn't hit an elephant at this dist—" as he was shot mid-sentence. I am hoping for better! There's something about paying attention to the words that someone says when they know that they will be leaving for a long time, or perhaps forever. They are normally a deep expression of that person's heart and desire. When leaving the kids in the morning as I go to work, I make sure they know that I love them. That can be a challenge when trying to get out to school, church or anywhere past the front door. A lot of the conversation can be "Where's your coat? Have you brushed your teeth? No you can't bring that!" and a hundred other things. In all of the busyness the most important thing for me is to remember to say "I love you." Words matter as they show what is important to the person saying them.

One of the accusations often aimed at pastors and teachers who preach the message of God's unmerited favour is that we somehow are disconnected from the reality of what the world is really like. It is said that we should be careful not to get people's hopes up because if whatever they are in faith for does not work out, they will only be disappointed. I wish that the people who have said this about Penny and I could walk for five minutes in our shoes. We share the same struggles as every other person. Sometimes I reflect back on my life and wonder if I had known what we were going to have to walk through, would I have stayed the course? Honestly I am not sure that I would have. All I can say is that we have found the grace each day to keep going, even in the middle of some desperately difficult and painful situations. Grace does not pretend that trouble does not exist and it does not deny challenge; grace is how we frame life. It is either though my own effort or through the lens of Jesus' finished work. For me it is really a question of authority and who or what has the final say.

In all that we have read about Jesus we need to remind ourselves that He is not oblivious to what life is like. We can make the dysfunction around us personal and blame ourselves for the mess. We do sometimes live in the consequences of our poor decisions, however the world that we live in is broken. There is pain, sickness, disease and all kinds of physical, emotional and spiritual brokenness, this touches us all. Can you imagine for a moment what it is like to face all of that without the promise that Jesus finishes His ministry with?

"I have said these things to you, that in me you may have peace. In the world you will have tribulation. But take heart; I have overcome the world."
John 16:33

Jesus was not denying that there would be trouble; He was denying that trouble would have the final place of authority in our lives. Here he uses the word *Peace - eiréné -* in Greek, which is translated *"wholeness and rest."* In a world of trouble and tribulation, the Holy Spirit in you is greater than anything that stands against the promises of God over your life. You can only live in that rest when you know who is in you is truly greater than that which is around you!

The statements that Jesus made about Himself were more than just nice things to read. They are powerful truths for you to live by today. When He said that He had "overcome" He used the word *tharseo -* which means *"properly, bolstered within which supports unflinching courage – literally, to radiate warm confidence."* Then the word "overcome" *is nik-ah'-o* from where we see the brand NIKE derive its name. It means victory *after* a battle. A battle is implied, but that is not your battle. You do not need to fight today, the struggle is not yours. Jesus is saying that all of the principalities, all the sin, all the mess, dysfunction, sickness, lack, and depravity of humanity is not for you to fight against. In yourself you are not equipped for that fight; in your own strength you will fail. He has faced these things on your behalf, grace has won the final victory. He went into battle and He won and now even death is defeated! That is the ultimate hope that we carry in our hearts today.

His heart for you

I want to finish this book in John 17 as this chapter is unparalleled in the Bible. It is unique among all the parts of scripture because it is the prayer between Jesus and His Father. The words are simple enough yet the truth of what He is saying is deeply profound. Chapters 13-16 record the words of Jesus to His disciples on the night of the Passover. This was the Thursday night of Passion Week, the night before His crucifixion. He spent hours with His disciples having the Passover meal. He led them in communion and continued to teach them. Chapter 17 is a prayer that He prays after this to His Father. We get a front row seat as we hear the depth of what is on Jesus' heart for us. He prays that the Father would fulfill all the promises He has made, and that He would bring to fulfillment all the work that He has done. This chapter has been called many different names - the Holy of Holies of Scripture, the prayer above all prayers and the 'real Lord's prayer.'

We see the communion between the Son of God and the Father. We see Jesus as our great high priest, the mediator between God and man. The prayer is divided into three parts. The first five verses, Jesus prays for Himself. And then starting in verse 6, He prays for the apostles that are with Him on that very night. Then He closes the chapter by praying for all believers throughout time. That includes you and me. Starting in verse 6, everything He prayed for the eleven He prays for all His people through all history. He starts by praying for His own glory, and then He prays for the glory of His own people:

"you have given him authority over all flesh, to give eternal life to all whom you have given him. And this is eternal life, that they know you, the only true God, and Jesus Christ whom you have sent."
John 17:2-3

This is such an amazing verse. Remember what we have been talking about in this journey. I started this book with a story of a young boy running for freedom; we run towards what we think will make us free. That's where we gravitate to. Every human heart is looking for freedom, for hope, for wholeness, for completeness. I was brought up thinking that this kind of life was only reserved for heaven, I had to die first before I could really live. I know that our ultimate hope is heaven and to be in the presence of Jesus however that is not what Jesus was only praying about here. Firstly He says that He is the only one with authority to give that kind of life. The word eternal in Greek is *ainos*, this was a real game changer for me.

A look at the Strong's definition tells us *"Aionos does not focus on the future per se, but rather on the quality of the age (165 /aiŏn) it relates to. Thus believers live in "eternal (166 /aiŏnios) life" right now, experiencing this quality of God's life now as a present possession."*

What an incredible truth. I remember discovering this as I studied and realising that Jesus prayed for me that I would experience God's quality of life now. All of the religion in me revolted as I thought that this could not be true. When I get to heaven I hope it will be so, but right now? What about my mistakes, doubts and failures? When we are confronted with a gap between our own experience and the word of God then what I have learned to do is to throw myself on grace and believe that there is more for me. I have seen the mess caused when we redefine who God is based on our own subjective experience. Grace lifts us up to see from a new perspective. We can declare that no matter what trouble we encounter in this world, Jesus has overcome it.

If Jesus did not mean that why did He say it? It is humbling to come to the point where we realise that we are not all "it." He is God and we are not. With our own limited understanding we will never work it all out or understand why some things happen. I do not want a God that fits neatly in a package of my understanding and experience. That would be no God at all. Although it is not always easy I want to find myself continually in that place of discovering the length, breadth, depth and height of the love of the eternal God. It causes hope to rise in my heart and encourages me that my best days are still to come.

"That they know you" is the word *ginóskō* ("experientially know") that I mentioned previously. God Life is not an academic subject or knowledge for the sake of it. What kind of relationship would that be where we hear about love but never feel it? When Jesus says *"The only true God..."* (*theós*) He used the word that means *"the supreme being who owns and sustains all things."* He is showing us the one who has ultimate authority. He is praying that you would experience His love and grace and that life would be the result. In that intimate moment between Father and Son you see His heart and desire for you. He is not cold, He is not uncaring, He is not uninterested, He is not condemning, He is not holding back and He is not far off.

We live in a world where there are lots of functional Gods. These are the things that demand our heart, affection and attention. These are where we put our trust, particularly when the pressure of life is coming in on us. As I said before, no matter what they promise they will never deliver. They are fake news. Jesus says that He is the only place where you will find a quality of God life that brings rest and wholeness in every part.

Hear how much He loves you

We live in a world full of significant challenge. I do not watch a lot of main stream media but when I do I am amazed at how negative it is.

It is easy to become overwhelmed with the enormity of what is going on around us. I love that we get to eavesdrop on this moment between Jesus and His Father. It brings us such hope that we can live securely.

Jesus prays that the Father would keep us safe in the world through the word of grace:

"I do not ask that you take them out of the world, but that you keep them from the evil one. They are not of the world, just as I am not of the world. Sanctify them in the truth; your word is truth."
John 17:15—17

Here we have a throwback to John 1:1 - it is the very same word for *Word*, Jesus Himself. If we paraphrase what Jesus is saying we see verse 17 means *"make them holy through my work, I am Alethia - divine truth revealed to man."*

There is so much more that I could say here as there are many books written on this chapter alone, the prayer of prayers. But I want to ask you to think and consider what you are going to do with what you have heard? We clearly see His heart for us. To know Jesus and His grace and from that place to live our lives so that we demonstrate the glory of God to the world. That's what He was praying. His promises to be with us and to protect us in the middle of trouble are there to be seen, His heart and love for you is on view. You do not need to be afraid or anxious about today, tomorrow or any other day. He has promised you God quality life in the middle of a crazy world!

That you may believe

Who do you say Jesus is? How you answer that question will impact on the quality of life that you live. It will profoundly impact your ability to live in faith for your future. We live in a different time but the parallels could not be more obvious. In our modern world people are searching for and investing in a thousand different things to help them find purpose and wholeness. Ultimately none of them will ever meet that need. Jesus showed the people that everything that they longed for would be found in Him. It did not require anything other than a humble heart and a posture of receiving.

I hope that you have been encouraged as you have read these chapters. My prayer is that you have see Jesus perhaps in a way that you have never seen Him before. Every single need in your life is met perfectly and completely in this revelation of Jesus. Each of these statements we have read together are individually powerful and collectively represent all that we need today. In this revelation we find life, real life. I want to encourage you not to leave these truths behind and move onto whatever will grab for your attention, but to allow the Lord Himself to write these truths deep into your heart. I pray that as your revelation of Jesus and His grace for you deepens, you would experience more of His life in and around you.

I'll leave you with our signature verse as for me it says it more perfectly than I ever could:

"But these are written that you may believe that Jesus is the Messiah, the Son of God, and that by believing you may have life in His name."
John 20:31

What happens now?

I hope that you have been encouraged as you have read this book. God loves you and He is for you. The most important decision that you will ever make is to give your life to Jesus and follow Him forever. If you have never prayed to become a follower of Jesus and you would like to I would encourage you to pray this prayer. Remember it's not the prayer that saves; it's the repentance and faith behind the prayer that matters!

"Lord Jesus, I come to you today, I know I'm a sinner and I cannot save myself, I ask that you forgive my sin and give me the gift of eternal life. I accept you as my Lord and Savior, come into my heart today, in Jesus' name."

You are not designed to live life alone. Can I encourage you to get a Bible and connect with a local church where you will be able to grow in your faith and discover more of the purpose that God has for your life.

We would also love to equip you with some great resources to help you grow in the love and grace of God.

Please contact us at: **office@exchangechurchbelfast.com**

About the Author

Andrew Toogood was born and bred in Northern Ireland and now lives in the heart of East Belfast. He is married to Penny and they have three great kids, Ben, Hope and Sophie, along with a beagle called Bella.

Andrew is the founder of Exchange Church Belfast, a church community established on the peace line in East Belfast. The heart and mission of Exchange is to see lives transformed by grace. The church is about leading people to discover the grace and unmerited favour of God that is only found in the finished work of Jesus. Andrew's heart is to see the fullness Jesus revealed so that lives can be lifted from condemnation into freedom.

Andrew is also an in demand leadership facilitator and speaker. He founded and leads Proclaim Consulting; a Leadership Development consultancy that trains and equips leaders and managers in organisations around the world. Proclaim works with leaders in Fortune 100 and FTSE 100 companies, as well as leading brands in industries including technology, banking, legal & professional services and many others. Proclaim have trained thousands of leaders and managers in the key competencies needed by individuals and organisations for success in a rapidly changing world.

You can connect with me on:

- 🌐 http://www.exchangechurchbelfast.com
- 🔗 http://www.proclaimconsulting.com
- 🔗 http://www.proclaimconsulting.academy

Printed in Great Britain
by Amazon